Anne Bradstreet Now

Anne Bradstreet Now

Modern Poets Respond

Edited by
ABRAM VAN ENGEN
MARY EYRING

OXFORD
UNIVERSITY PRESS

OXFORD
UNIVERSITY PRESS

Oxford University Press is a department of the University of Oxford.
It furthers the University's objective of excellence in research, scholarship,
and education by publishing worldwide. Oxford is a registered trade mark of
Oxford University Press in the UK and in certain other countries.

Published in the United States of America by Oxford University Press
198 Madison Avenue, New York, NY 10016, United States of America.

CIP data is on file at the Library of Congress

ISBN 9780197811160 (pbk.)
ISBN 9780197811153 (hbk.)

DOI: 10.1093/9780197811191.001.0001

Paperback printed by Marquis Book Printing, Canada
Hardback printed by Lightning Source, Inc., United States of America

The manufacturer's authorized representative in the EU for product safety is
Oxford University Press España S.A. of Parque Empresarial San Fernando de Henares,
Avenida de Castilla, 2 – 28830 Madrid (www.oup.es/en or product.safety@oup.com).
OUP España S.A. also acts as importer into Spain of products made by the manufacturer.

FSC www.fsc.org MIX Paper | Supporting responsible forestry FSC® C103567

Contents

Anne Bradstreet Today

In 1650, the puritan poet Anne Bradstreet became the first person from British North America to publish a book of poems. *The Tenth Muse Lately Sprung Up in America*, published in London, made her famous. Back in New England, Anne Bradstreet continued writing until her death in 1672, but no further poem appeared in print during her lifetime. Six years after she died, John Foster in Boston published a second edition of her works, which was "enlarged by an addition of several other poems found amongst her papers after her death."[1] These two books circulated for centuries, along with Bradstreet's manuscripts, and in 1867 even more of her writings entered print under the guiding hand of John Harvard Ellis. When anthologies of American literature began appearing in the early twentieth century, Anne Bradstreet became newly positioned as a founder, a first, a poet who paved the way for American poets yet to come. Today, several editions of her complete works vie for attention. Meanwhile, eagerness for Anne abides. A digital project (findinganne.org) continues searching for materials, while the buried ruins of her burnt house in Andover have just been uncovered. Anne Bradstreet keeps emerging. Printed and circulated, canonized and anthologized, studied and taught, scrutinized and enjoyed, Bradstreet has been part of American culture for almost four centuries.

Each generation discovers their own Anne Bradstreet. Early readers saw in her works the piety of a housewife who accepted her role in society and conformed her life to the dictates and expectations of puritan society. Later readers highlighted a seemingly rebellious spirit crying out from an early American outpost. Poems like "The Prologue" and Bradstreet's elegy to Queen Elizabeth, in addition to the learning of her longer poems and her engagements with English politics, all seem to suggest a person less constrained by piety and more disciplined by strategy—a feminist spirit navigating puritan norms. More recently, Bradstreet has been portrayed as a reluctant immigrant, one whose heart rose at the sight of the American

[1] See Anne Bradstreet, *Poems and Meditations*, ed. Margaret Olofson Thickstun (Toronto: Iter Press, 2019).

shore, while still others see in her work worldviews of the settler-colonists who occupied others' land and then attempted to erase and replace those who lived there. Native Americans, who dwelt in close proximity with Anne Bradstreet, make no appearance in her writings. Through the years, and still today, some readers have been drawn to her various modes of spiritual devotion. Whatever the approach to Anne Bradstreet, her works repeatedly demand a response.

The current book takes up that demand in a fresh way. Here, the voices of modern poets respond to the writings of Anne Bradstreet. Their creative work complements the dedicated scholarship of past decades, offering a different angle into understanding Anne. The poets who lent their work to this volume were asked to write something in poetry or prose related to any aspect of Bradstreet's work. Some have been interested in Bradstreet all their lives and careers. Others encountered Bradstreet's poetry and meditations for the first time because of our invitation. Their responses suggest that while it is possible for contemporary poets to be unfamiliar with Bradstreet's work, it is unlikely they will be unaffected by the experience of reading it. Some are moved directly, while others indirectly feel their way to what might be moving for others. Yet even to feel estranged by her puritan faith, her cultural elitism, or the rigidity of her rhymed couplets is to be transported in its own way. Bradstreet's work indexes the differences between her world and ours, but it also illuminates tissues—some twinging with pain—that connect us still.

While Bradstreet has remained in print since the seventeenth century, her popularity has waxed and waned, often in tandem with the tides of critical interest. The idea for this book picks up from the revival of Anne Bradstreet that happened in the mid-twentieth century. At that time, two prominent poets focused attention on Bradstreet's life and works through their own poetry and prose. First, John Berryman wrote a 57-stanza curious and complicated ode called *Homage to Mistress Bradstreet*. In many ways, he made his name on that poem. (In this collection, you will find some poets combining Berryman and Bradstreet in their response.) A decade later, the poet and activist Adrienne Rich introduced the complete works of Anne Bradstreet for an edition that remains in print even now, sold every year to new students in countless classrooms across the country. Yet Bradstreet's audience has always extended beyond America, and in recent years, the well-known Irish poet Eavan Boland took up Bradstreet once again. Inspired by Berryman, Rich, and Boland, we have gathered leading poets to write and reflect on Bradstreet's writings—her voice, her strains, her harmonies and disharmonies, her influence and legacy, her past and foreign strangeness, as well as her present and lasting resonance.[2]

Such work fits well with recent moves in early American literature and American Studies more generally. Over the past two decades, scholars and teachers have hungrily sought materials that will link early America more directly to the present day. Classes on early American culture now regularly incorporate contemporary creative writers and their works—such as *A Mercy* by Toni Morrison or *The Age of Phillis* by Honorée Fanonne Jeffers. Some instructors assign film adaptations and other historical novels (like *Caleb's Crossing* or *Year of Wonders* by Geraldine Brooks), asking students to set primary texts from the 1600s against modern re-imaginations of early America. In keeping with such moves, Patrick Erben and Rebecca Harrison have just released a book called *Early America and the Modern Imagination: Rewriting the Past in the Present.*[3] Beyond new classes, new course materials, and new books, the main scholarly society of early American literature (the Society of Early Americanists) now runs presentations of creative writers at their academic conference every year. The past lives in the present—and sometimes creative writers are best at showing us how.

When we approached several prominent poets in America, asking them to think and write about Anne Bradstreet's work and world, their response was enthusiastic—even more so than we anticipated. The collected accomplishments of those included here are astounding: winners of the National Book Award and the National Book Critics Circle Award, a MacArthur winner, and a whole litany of other top prizes in poetry—far too many to list (see the contributors' bios). Suffice it to say that these are some of the most accomplished poets in America today, and they all took up the invitation to write in response to Anne Bradstreet.

[2] John Berryman, *Homage to Mistress Bradstreet* (New York: Farrar, Straus, and Giroux, 1956); Adrienne Rich, "Anne Bradstreet and Her Poetry," foreword in *Anne Bradstreet: The Works of Anne Bradstreet*, ed. Jeannine Hensley (Cambridge: Belknap, 1967); Eavan Boland, "Finding Anne Bradstreet," in *Green Thoughts, Green Shades: Essays by Contemporary Poets on the Early Modern Lyric*, ed. Jonathan F.S. Post (Berkeley: University of California Press, 2002), 176–190; Eavan Boland, "Becoming Anne Bradstreet," from *Shakespeare's Sisters: Women Writers Bridge Five Centuries*, ed. Gigi Bradford et al. (Washington, D.C.: Folger Shakespeare Library, 2012).

[3] Toni Morrison, *A Mercy* (New York: Vintage, 2009); Honorée Fanonne Jeffers, *The Age of Phillis* (Middletown, CT: Wesleyan University Press, 2020); Geraldine Brooks, *Year of Wonders* (New York: Penguin, 2002); Geraldine Brooks, *Caleb's Crossing* (New York: Penguin, 2011); Patrick Erben and Rebecca Harrison, *Early America and the Modern Imagination: Rewriting the Past in the Present* (Edinburgh: Edinburgh University Press, 2025).

To ensure variety, we have brought together a diverse array of poets. They represent different genders, orientations, backgrounds, perspectives, religions, and races. Moreover, the stylistic approach diverges significantly from poet to poet. Some value accessibility and clarity, while others move through more experimental modes and alternative techniques. Some work with narrative while others dig with lyric. Some wrote essays; some wrote poems. Formal and informal, faith-based and otherwise, white, Black, Latinx, Indigenous, and Asian American—the volume allows for multiple approaches to Bradstreet through many different angles and tactics, reflecting diversity at the level of writer, response, style, method, mood, and more.

The parameters for these poets were simple: write anything you like in response to Bradstreet's world and work. Poets could spin lyrics from a single verse Bradstreet left behind, or they could tie together themes from several poems across her work. They could meditate on Bradstreet's meditations, or they could pick out a thread woven throughout her poetry. Each artist was invited to write something fresh—a poem, an essay, or both—each in their own style and voice. The results are remarkable. The range, the inspirations, the approaches all give readers a fresh way to navigate, enter, and understand the poetry and prose of Anne Bradstreet. In the work of modern poets, we receive Anne Bradstreet anew.

Anne Bradstreet

But who was Anne Bradstreet? To answer that question, we have to scrap together bits and pieces of information from a sparse set of papers. The records of Anne Bradstreet are a meager lot. We have more poems and meditations than biographical details and data. We do not even know when she was born. It was either 1612 or 1613, but that date is itself gleaned from a poem she wrote and dated in 1632.

We do know, however, that Anne Bradstreet was born into a relatively good situation. Her father, Thomas Dudley, served as a law clerk to Judge Nicolls in Northamptonshire and then, more prominently, became steward to the Earl of Lincoln, Theophilus Fiennes-Clinton. Dudley did what few others could do: he put the estate in order. Dudley rescued the Earl of Lincoln from enormous debts and helped stabilize the house. In such a role, his children received many of the aristocracy's benefits. Anne lived well in the Sempringham Manor.

More importantly, such living meant that Anne grew up with books. Training for literacy would have begun around the age of four, and studies would have extended and expanded until the time of her marriage in 1628. We know that girls were not excluded from study in the house.[4] And we know, as well, that Anne took to her learning with some avidity and delight. Her absorption of knowledge appears throughout her works.[5] The subject of history seemed especially compelling to her, structuring as it does her longest set of poems, but many other topics also consumed her attention: modern science, anatomy, theology, philosophy, and politics. In the house of a great lord, with a large library at her disposal, supported by her father and family, Anne filled her mind and time with books.

Such learning suited the circles in which her family moved. Her father and the Earl of Lincoln both supported puritan causes, and puritans valued literacy and higher learning. For them, as the scholar Alec Ryrie has written, "Ignorance, like illiteracy, was innocent if you could not help it, but if you had opportunities for learning and spurned them, woe betide you."[6] When numerous puritans sailed to New England, therefore, they established schools almost immediately. They passed laws requiring education. They built a new college (Harvard). They brought a printing press. And they imported large libraries. Anne came to New England in 1630, at the age of eighteen, and she would live her entire adult life far from the early aristocratic halls of England, but she would never be separated from books. Because her ongoing studies inform her writing so extensively, Bradstreet has been described as "fundamentally an intellectual writer": according to Margaret Olofson Thickstun, "The preponderance of her poetry engages with books, not experience, with

[4] As Laura Lunger Knoppers explains, "Educational spaces for girls . . . were often found within the household, moving the humanist classroom (from which girls were largely excluded) into domestic education, enhanced in the everyday work of household business, receipts and financial transactions. Although women's best place was said to be in the home, the early modern household . . . was a space of considerable authority, anxiety and fantasy for its residents." Knoppers, "Introduction: Critical Framework and Issues," in *Cambridge Companion to Early Modern Women's Writing*, ed. Laura Lunger Knoppers (New York: Cambridge University Press, 2009), 11.

[5] As the biographer Elizabeth Wade White has written, "The character and extent of her studies can best be judged by an examination of her writings, which are so varied in subject and so filled with the materials of learning that one wonders how, in those eleven growing years, she managed to absorb so much knowledge and retain it so well in her memory." White, *Anne Bradstreet: The Tenth Muse* (New York: Oxford University Press, 1971), 60.

[6] Alec Ryrie, *Being Protestant in Reformation Britain* (Oxford: Oxford University Press, 2013), 263.

ideas, not feelings."[7] That is somewhat debatable, but what remains unarguable is that book-learning and extensive study made possible Bradstreet's poetry.

It helped, then, that Anne always lived among the elite. While literacy might have been required (or hoped) of all, few in puritan New England actually owned a library or had access to one. Schools might teach basic literacy, but they did not train farmers to leave their station and join the intellectual class. Most people did not have time or ability to expand their learning beyond basic reading, writing, and arithmetic. Engaging with scripture on one's own might be essential to salvation, and it might remain an expected part of daily life, but reading more than holy writ was never strictly necessary. It took a little status to explore much beyond the bible and the basics of godly living.

Anne Bradstreet had status. Her father, Thomas Dudley, served as a magistrate in New England and one of the earliest governors of Massachusetts Bay. For Anne, Thomas seemed to have been a stable support, an encouragement to learning and growth, a spur to writing, a poetic competitor, and an important influence throughout her life. For others, Dudley could be a difficult disciplinarian, something of an inflexible tyrant with a narrow view of the law. As the biographer Elizabeth Wade White summarizes, "His stern adherence to principle made him a pillar of strength to the young colony, as well as a symbol of bigoted intolerance to those who disagreed with him."[8] Even Anne, in tributes penned to her father, seemed to acknowledge that he had a knack for accruing enemies.

At first landing, Anne, with her husband Simon, settled with Thomas Dudley in Newtowne (what would later become Cambridge). They remained there five years, during which time Anne's first child, Samuel, was born. In 1635, Anne and Simon, along with most of their extended family members, removed to Ipswich—a newer town about forty miles north of Boston. Over the next decade, several more children would arrive, while Thomas Dudley would be called off as governor and Simon Bradstreet would be sent away

[7] Margaret Olofson Thickstun, "Introduction," in Anne Bradstreet, *Poems and Meditations*, ed. Margaret Olofson Thickstun (Toronto: Iter, 2019), 14.

[8] White, *Anne Bradstreet*, 5. Marilyn Westerkamp offers this portrait of Thomas Dudley: "For all his power and stature, Thomas Dudley, an authoritarian, irascible, righteous magistrate, was an essentially simple man. Gifted with neither the wisdom of the serpent nor the harmlessness of the dove, Dudley displayed the intuitive instinct that often accompanies an uncomplicated mind." Westerkamp, *The Passion of Anne Hutchinson: An Extraordinary Woman, the Puritan Patriarchs, and the World They Made and Lost* (New York: Oxford University Press, 2021), 27.

repeatedly on government duties. All this while, Anne Bradstreet wrote—including some occasional verse ("Upon a Fit of Sickness"), some elegies (to Queen Elizabeth and her mother, for example), and some much longer poems that cascade down the page in heroic couplets.

In 1645, the Bradstreets moved once more, becoming one of the first English families in the new puritan colonial settlement of Andover, about fifteen miles west and inland from Ipswich. As with Ipswich, the land had been previously cleared and settled by Native Americans for plantings.[9] During each of her removes, Anne wrote, studied, birthed children (she had eight eventually), raised children (all of whom lived to adulthood), and ran a large household while her husband frequently traveled. Always tied to the elite, Anne had close relations with ministers and magistrates in Boston, Cambridge, Ipswich, and Andover. The current of her conversation flowed through the latest imported books. And the more she wrote, the more praise and honor she seemed to receive.

Such praise came to new heights with the publication of her poetry. From the small village of Andover (now North Andover), which was set alongside the Merrimack River in Massachusetts Bay, her brother-in-law John Woodbridge took a manuscript of her works—a presentation copy which Bradstreet may have prepared for circulation among local readers—and sailed for England in 1647. There he engaged the printer Stephen Bowtell and facilitated the publication of *The Tenth Muse Lately Sprung Up in America*, the first book of poetry by an American writer. Bradstreet always disavowed any intention to put her poetry in print, and to this day scholars do not know whether she gave Woodbridge the manuscript (and if she did, whether she merely meant for him to share it with English friends) or whether he took it without her knowledge.

The publication of *The Tenth Muse* has secured Anne Bradstreet's place in history, where she is often called "the first American poet" (try searching that phrase online, for example). But of course, Anne Bradstreet was not the first. The first poets in America practiced their art long before a country

[9] As Thickstun writes, "The Massachusetts Bay colonists benefited from arriving in land that had been managed for centuries, with abandoned garden plots and cleared meadows surrounding seasonal village sites." Thickstun, "Introduction," 9. The land for Andover had been sold to the English by Cutshamekin, sachem of the Massachusett, on May 6, 1646, part of a broader realignment of sovereignty in the region. For more on the sovereignty claims, contestations, violence, and strategies of English and Native encounters at this time and in his region, see Jenny Hale Pulsipher, *Subjects unto the Same King: Indians, English, and the Contest for Authority in Colonial New England* (Philadelphia, University of Pennsylvania Press, 2014).

called "England" even existed. They passed their poetics from one generation to another over many millennia. When Bradstreet stepped on American shores, she entered a terrain rich with poetry and poetic practice—in storytelling and oral arts—that was often engaged and carried forward by women. The ground had been fruitfully tilled, though the English did not recognize it. Anne Bradstreet's voice added her own flavor to a much wider and longer-lived American harvest of verse.

Not only can Bradstreet not be considered the "first" American poet; she also can hardly be considered "American." We must remember, as Anne never forgot, that she was first and foremost English. She saw herself connected to a homeland across the sea, and her poetry would suggest that such a place never drifted far from her mind. As various commentators have pointed out, New England scenery (let alone the Indigenous inhabitants of America) never makes an appearance in her work.[10] Anne Bradstreet, like most puritans of New England, looked east.

The closest we come to the sense of an American identity arises in Bradstreet's political poem of 1642 on the English dissensions that were then driving toward civil war. Again, the subject was England, not America. The politics of her homeland concerned her deeply, though she lived at the time in Ipswich. The perspective of the poem, "A Dialogue Between Old England and New," definitively gives the upper hand to New England, the American colony—the daughter who has all the answers for her mother's woe. Apart from that one poem, however, little else in all the works of Bradstreet would suggest that her writings came from one side of the Atlantic or the other. Anne Bradstreet was not so much an *American* poet as an early modern *English* poet living in Massachusetts Bay.

So much was Anne Bradstreet English that her poetry participated in the colonizing project of the early English puritans. And that, too, must never be forgotten. Bradstreet projected English authority over America, in part by ignoring the inhabitants of America and in part by refusing to acknowledge or register the ways America might change her work or challenge her world.[11] While theories abound about why Woodbridge actually took Bradstreet's poems to England and had them published, most suggestions

[10] As Thickstun writes, "Nowhere in her poems does she describe a landscape that could be located in a particular space, let alone North America." Thickstun, "Introduction," 15.

[11] As Tamara Harvey has written, poets like Anne Bradstreet "used the objectifying rhetoric of commerce and empire to authorize their own poetic voices." Harvey, "'My Goods Are True': Tenth Muses in the New World Market," *Feminist Interventions in Early American Studies*, ed. Mary Carruth (Tuscaloosa: University of Alabama Press, 2006), 18.

circle around the way her book might have been used to elevate the colonial cause. *The Tenth Muse* showed off an American woman's talents and abilities to an English audience. Wrapped in seeming orthodoxy and submission, Anne Bradstreet demonstrated extraordinary education and refinement. That, too, contributed to the colony's needs and claims. Under such a guise, the Elizabethan past becomes an idyllic construct Bradstreet imports to American shores.[12] As Phillip Round notes, first-generation puritan New Englanders like Bradstreet were often "forced to reach out and perform saintliness, Englishness, trustworthiness, and marketability to a metropolitan audience, using the recognized public gestures of civil conversation."[13] *The Tenth Muse* accomplished all such ends. Anne Bradstreet practiced English poetics, insisting on her English identity all the more fervently the further she found herself physically removed from England itself.

Puritanism

While Anne Bradstreet was definitively English all her life, that English identity came marked by a distinct strain of puritanism. And English puritanism took its own forms again as it was lived and experienced in the contours of New England. To understand what made Anne Bradstreet who she was, and even why she found herself in Massachusetts Bay, we must grasp a basic sense of what defined and drove the puritan cause.

Puritans arose out of the Reformation as a group of zealous Protestants who wanted to see further reforms in the Church of England. When the Church of England broke from Catholicism in 1534 under Henry VIII (who reigned 1509-1547), it retained many Catholic rites and practices. After the brief reign of the young Protestant King Edward VI (1547-1553), Mary I took over as Queen of England, ruling from 1553 to 1558. During those five years, she tried to return the country to Catholicism, and since she targeted Protestant leaders, many of them fled. Some of those English reformers ended up in Geneva, sitting at the feet of John Calvin (1509-1564).

[12] As Christopher D'Addario writes, "By calling on Elizabethan forebears, Bradstreet evokes not a direct connection with the homeland that she had left behind, and for whom her works were published, but instead a nostalgic distance from current affairs that connects her with a purer past era." D'Addario, *Exile and Journey in Seventeenth-Century Literature* (Cambridge: Cambridge University Press, 2007), 44.

[13] Phillip Round, *By Nature and By Custom Cursed: Transatlantic Civil Discourse and New England Cultural Production, 1620–1660* (Hanover: University Press of New England, 1999), 15.

When Queen Elizabeth I took the throne in 1558 (ruling until 1603), she declared England Protestant once again, and leading reformers returned from the European mainland with even greater enthusiasm for Calvinist theology and practice. Queen Elizabeth tried to moderate between the extremes of Protestantism on offer, but over the course of her 45-year reign, a subset of Protestants kept pushing for greater reforms. Although they were not part of a single ecclesiastical body, these Protestants were called puritans, or quite frequently "nonconformists" (because they refused to conform to the structures, practices, or requirements of the Church of England).

Under the reign of King James I (1603-1625), the puritans pressed their case more and more. James both accommodated and resisted them. His son, however, was far less forgiving. With Charles I on the throne (1625-1649), puritans became newly targeted by the church and government, often silenced, and sometimes imprisoned. For many reasons (not just his anti-puritanism), the rule of Charles resulted in a great deal of backlash and resistance. In the 1640s, civil war broke out across England, leading finally to the beheading of the Archbishop of the Church of England (in 1645) and King Charles himself (in 1649). From 1649 to 1660, England had no monarch. Instead, the country was ruled by the Lord Protector Oliver Cromwell, who led the armies against King Charles.

That context defines Anne Bradstreet's life. Under the rule of Charles I, her father, Thomas Dudley, found himself in danger. His employer, the Earl of Lincoln, had openly disobeyed King Charles in defense of puritan principles (refusing to pay one of the King's forced loans), and the King had sent the Earl to prison. Dudley, a fellow puritan and nonconformist, faced an angry monarch "as the known retainer and counsellor of a man of substance and title who had dared to defy the king's edict."[14] That was in 1627. Two years later, plans had been put in place to leave. By 1630, Dudley, with his young assistant Simon Bradstreet (whom Anne had married in 1628) and many other prominent puritans, had sold their goods and set their sights on New England.

Puritans, then, were those who challenged the Church of England to reform its ways. They often had different (and sometimes rather definitive) ideas about how authority ought to be structured and distributed in the church, and toward what ends it ought (or ought not) be used. They opposed whatever smacked of "men's inventions"—that is, whatever ceremonies and

[14] White, *Anne Bradstreet*, 82.

rites they thought had arisen without sufficient biblical basis. In their eyes, they were seeking to return the church to its pure original form, scraping away the debris of traditions and rituals that had accumulated through past ages of corrupt Christianity.[15]

In pursuing such ends, puritans frequently sought one another out. They banded together in tight communities of faithful reformers. An intense pursuit of communion with God defined the community of the so-called "godly." In the interest of that pursuit, puritans called together separate conferences or "conventicles" within their wider parishes (an early form of church small groups); they attended similar schools together (especially Emmanuel College, Cambridge); and they traveled together to hear the preaching of select "godly" ministers (called "sermon gadding"). In that sense, puritan community often involved a physical separation from the "ungodly" through practices of gathering and gadding. But in addition to physical separation, puritanism also placed a mental distance between the "godly" and the "ungodly." Puritans frequently perceived themselves as a persecuted minority fighting for the true church and pursuing the righteous cause of God.

That cause turned on a distinct notion and practice of piety. The saints, in Calvinist theology, were those chosen by God for salvation before the foundations of the world. Such a belief in predestination did not make choices in life less fraught or the experience of free will any less burdened. Rather, each choice made in life could serve to *reveal* the status of one's eternal soul—whether someone was a saint (destined for heaven) or a reprobate (destined for hell). Good works could not *produce* or *earn* salvation (salvation could only be received as a gift), but righteous and godly living could carry weight as a sign and seal of grace.

The presence of grace, meanwhile, was known primarily by its *experience*. Puritans practiced an emotional religion—or, to be more precise, a religion that depended on movements of the heart. Sorrow (for sin) and joy (at forgiveness) were expected aspects of godly living. And both aspects appear, quite naturally, in the poetry of Anne Bradstreet. She lived the ups and downs that puritanism built into its "practical divinity"—its guide for godly living. Puritanism, in other words, was not just a set of doctrines or positions

[15] For the foundational book explaining this driving desire of puritanism, see Theodore Dwight Bozeman, *The Precisianist Strain: Disciplinary Religion and Antinomian Backlash in Puritanism to 1638* (Chapel Hill: University of North Carolina Press, 2004).

forcefully asserted or mentally accepted. Instead, puritanism constituted a way of life aimed at the experience of grace.

Contrary to public perception, therefore, puritans did not hate happiness, punish joy, wear all-black clothes, hate sex, or enforce arcane and rigid laws for the pure sake of discipline and rigidity. Instead, as Marilyn Westerkamp has written, the puritan community was "permeated with joyous piety, where spiritual gifts were understood and holiness admired."[16] A kind of mysticism flowed naturally from puritan theology. Communion with God remained a persistent goal of godly living, and for many, that communion with God was experienced most richly in what puritans called the "love of the brethren"—those strong, communal bonds within the church that carried over from English conventicles.[17]

Such joyous communions did not mean that all puritans thrived, or that life was easy, or that doubts, fears, afflictions, and punishments were absent. The darker aspects of puritanism persisted as well, and all these features and experiences can be found in the writings of Anne Bradstreet. Puritans conceived of the love of God and love of neighbor in ways that left many neighbors out cold. And because puritans valued community so highly, they often, quite intentionally, bound it tightly *against* the broader society, assuming outsiders in order to create a minority of insiders. That feature of puritanism became especially fraught in New England, where the puritans ruled and tried to establish a godly society for all, while still carving out a special sanctum of the godly within.

Yet for all their love of community—and for all the ways one's love of the right community in the right way might reveal the status of one's soul—ultimately puritans stood bare and alone before a mighty, mysterious, and sovereign God. A turn to the self came naturally in puritan theology. The autobiography was certainly not invented by puritans, but the puritans of New England practiced regularly the art of reading signs in one's life and telling it back to others as a story of grace (or its absence). Such a practice informs much of the lyric poetry that Anne Bradstreet produced. She searches her life. She interprets it. She narrates events and discovers meaning in each new development, weaving together a plotline that moves back and forth from sin and sorrow to grace and joy.

[16] Westerkamp, *The Passion of Anne Hutchinson*, 4.

[17] For more on this concept and its centrality to puritanism, see Abram Van Engen, *Sympathetic Puritans: Calvinist Fellow-Feeling in Early New England* (New York: Oxford University Press, 2015).

In her first of 77 meditations, penned for her children, Anne Bradstreet clearly articulates the basic principle behind this entire philosophy of life: "There is no object that we see," she writes, "no action that we do, no good that we enjoy, no evil that we feel or fear, but we may make some spiritual advantage of all; and he that makes such improvement is wise as well as pious."[18] In other words, all of life is both a message and an opportunity. Every event is a sign. All sickness is a chance to grow in grace. At every point, the "wise" person looks for the hand of God and responds accordingly. Puritan writers did not believe in creating meaning out of the world they encountered, but rather in creatively using all they knew to *discover* and *disclose* the hand of God at work. Their theology called for constant observation and interpretation. Meaning, *deep meaning*, supported all and could always be found with the right godly practice and skill.

The fact that God worked in and through all things also meant that the world itself could never, in itself, be bad. It was not evil as such. The physical did not delineate the sinful. Instead, a good Creator-God had created a good world, and a love of the world was one way in which to experience and understand the love of God. It is true, as plenty of puritans preached, that the world could be loved *too much*: it might be idolized; it might be worshiped and loved *in place of* God. And if that occurred, it would indeed be problematic. To worship the world was to forget the Maker of the world. But hating the world was no sign of loving God, for God had given the world as a gift. To reject the goodness of the world was to reject its Maker. Accordingly, all loves had to be properly ordered, one love leading to the next, and all loves leading ultimately to God.

When Anne Bradstreet laments the burning of her house in a late poem, therefore, sin has nothing to do with it. The burning of the house did not result from sin, nor was a love of the house a sin, nor was grief for the loss of the house a sin. It was, instead, an affliction—a pain, or a tragedy, that came to saints and could be used to turn their loves even more thoroughly to God. As with any loss, the proper response was to ask how it might lead into further and deeper spiritual communion. In the case of this poem, Anne comes to realize that for all her love of the house, it was still just a house. It was always bound to pass. Her love for that house pointed to something beyond it,

[18] Anne Bradstreet, *Poems and Meditations*, ed. Margaret Olofson Thickstun (Toronto: Iter, 2019), 287.

something lasting, a longing for a joy that would never pass away. And so, as the poem concludes, she turns to an eternal home: "Thou hast an house on high erect / Framed by that mighty Architect / With glory richly furnished, / Stands permanent though this be fled" (ll. 43–46).[19] Notice, however, that a "house on high erect" could never offer comfort unless a *house* was itself something that could be loved. The puritans loved this world. *Through* their love of the world, they came to know, take comfort in, and long for the greater and more lasting love of God.[20]

Puritan Women

How such loves played out for puritan women constitutes a large and lively topic of conversation. Those who study the period debate whether puritanism raised the status of women or lowered it. No one contests that the period perceived women as subordinate to men in the social and political realms, although some add that the patriarchal nature of puritanism could make such subjection worse. Others, however, contend that puritanism elevated women by equalizing their spiritual status. Women, too, could draw close to God—and, moreover, their experiences could teach many others how to draw near as well. In addition, puritans often pictured the spiritual life in feminized terms, speaking of the soul as the bride of Christ and eroticizing the experience of union with Christ.[21]

The paradox of puritan women—praised and elevated on the one hand, scrutinized and subordinated on the other—can be seen especially well in the very different lives and outcomes of Anne Bradstreet and Anne Hutchinson, two women whose lives cross in the confines of the Massachusetts Bay Colony at the same time. Both were brilliant. Both were pious puritans and devoted mothers. Both could be sharp-tongued and witty. Both offered quick and cutting retorts to those who tried to put a woman in her place

[19] See Anne Bradstreet, "In Silent Night, When Rest I Took," in Bradstreet, *Poems and Meditations*, 337.

[20] For a longer discussion of the ways Bradstreet's faith integrated her investments in material and spiritual worlds, see Mary Eyring, *Saltwater: Grief in Early America* (Williamsburg, VA and Chapel Hill, NC: Omohundro Institute of Early American History and Culture and University of North Carolina Press, 2025), 49–63.

[21] This paragraph borrows from Abram C. Van Engen, "Puritanism," in *Oxford Bibliographies Online: Atlantic History*, ed. Trevor Burnard (Oxford and New York: Oxford University Press). That article also sketches out a series of scholarly works on this topic ("Puritanism and Women") as well as many other aspects of puritanism.

or questioned a woman's intellectual ability. Yet where Bradstreet rose, Hutchinson sank. Interpreting scripture in her home, teaching its meanings to women and men in ways that sometimes countered and critiqued ministerial authorities, Hutchinson drew the ire of powerful magistrates and became associated—fairly or not—with a series of political fissures threatening the fledgling colony. In the trials of Hutchinson, she was accused of usurping her husband's place (among other crimes). Over the course of two trials, she was eventually excommunicated from the church and banished from the colony.

Those who participated in the trials of Anne Hutchinson included Anne Bradstreet's own husband and father. Thomas Dudley served as deputy governor of the Bay Colony during Hutchinson's examination by the General Court in November 1637. He blamed Hutchinson for "vent[ing] divers of her strange opinions" and ascribed the lion's share of the colony's political turmoil to her potent influence. "[I]t being found that Mrs. Hutchinson is she that hath . . . been the cause of what is fallen out," he proposed, "why we must take away the foundation and the building will fall."[22] When Hutchinson defended the conventicles she hosted in her home as a "free will offering" of her time and resources, Simon Bradstreet retorted, "If it be a free will offering you ought to forbear it because it gives offense."[23] Hutchinson, having never written a word, found herself exiled for the ways she interpreted scripture and taught it to others—for the power of her words. Bradstreet, meanwhile, proved her learning and engaged in English politics, but puritan men praised her as a housewife, celebrated her as a poet, and promoted her as an American muse.

What did Anne Bradstreet make of this? What did she think of Anne Hutchinson? How did she respond to her husband and father—and to all the other magistrates who perceived Anne Hutchinson as a threat? Did she agree with them? Did she serve their cause and hope for Hutchinson's exile? Or did she bite her tongue and slip a sense of rebellion into her poetry and prose? We do not know. Bradstreet never left a single word of writing about Anne Hutchinson.

Scholars make sense of the Bradstreet-Hutchinson divide in various ways, but most seem to agree that—at least in appearance—Bradstreet's words could be used to support the New England Way, whereas Hutchinson's

[22] David D. Hall, *The Antinomian Controversy, 1636–1638: A Documentary History* (Durham, NC: Duke University Press), 317–18.

[23] Ibid.

teachings overtly challenged it. Whether Bradstreet actually supported all that puritans were about is itself a matter for ongoing debate. In her lifetime, however, Bradstreet's words did not spur a group of followers to resist false preachers, register repeated concerns with government officials, or petition magistrates to undo the punishments they had meted out. All of that, eventually, would be laid (unfairly) at the feet of Hutchinson. The speaking out of women was always dangerous, even potentially for Bradstreet, but the content and consequences of that speech—especially how it could be interpreted or used by others—determined in great measure how the women were viewed.[24]

Bradstreet and Hutchinson, after all, were not the only outspoken women in the early modern era. Over the last three decades, a host of fields have changed how we understand early modern women's writing, transatlantic puritanism, book history, manuscript culture, English politics, and the New England conditions of settler colonialism. Through the Society for the History of Authorship, Reading, and Publishing (founded in 1992), scholars have opened to view a whole world of women writers in the 1600s—along with their various publics and different forms of literary engagement. Old accounts of Anne Bradstreet often portray her as a singular female voice speaking up from a woman's presumed silence—a brilliant, lone poet in a puritan age. Recent scholarship changes that picture. Anne Bradstreet was brilliant, certainly, but her voice joined a chorus of women writing and speaking throughout the period.

The Puritan Culture of Letters

Early modern writing took distinct forms, especially for the puritans. In their constant search for the message behind everything, puritans deployed a whole series of broader English genres and literary styles in their own way. Three in particular engaged Anne Bradstreet: spiritual autobiography, meditation, and poetry.

Puritan spiritual autobiographies each built on a fundamental paradox. On the one hand, they had to identify a unique saint with a particular and individual life who had somehow received and perceived the grace of God.

[24] For a good overview of the misogyny of the period, see Westerkamp, *The Passion of Anne Hutchinson*, chapter 3.

On the other hand, puritans preached against the exaltation of the self (a sure sign of pride and sinfulness) and instead tried to follow given patterns of grace, conforming their lives to a generic narrative of godliness. We see both in Bradstreet. As she writes at the start of her own autobiography, "I have not studied in this you read to show my skill, but to declare the truth, not to set forth myself, but the glory of God." What follows is a setting forth of her own particular life and struggles in order to reveal the glory of God and her knowledge of grace. She frequently noted her desire to be remembered. She left her writings to her children, as she said, "That being gone, here you may find / What was your living mother's mind." As she tried to conform her life to patterns of grace, she also deployed a strong individual voice and asked to be remembered as a very particular self.

Unlike autobiographies, meditations drew the godly closer to God through a kind of mystic piety. Akin to aphorisms, each meditation nourished the spiritual life with a particular nugget of wisdom. Arising out of prayer, contemplation, and worship, they could be written down and circulated to other godly in the community. Mothers often passed spiritual wisdom to their children. Anne Bradstreet's own writings joined a much larger, longer, and very popular English tradition of the "mother's legacy," which constituted a mother's advice to her children (usually conjoined with her impending death). One of the most popular books of the age, for example, was Dorothy Leigh's *A Mother's Legacy* (1616).[25] In a similar vein, Anne Bradstreet frames her own meditations with her coming death. Writing to her son Simon, she explains: "You once desired me to leave something for you in writing that you might look upon when you should see me no more." Under the guise of a "mother's legacy," Anne Bradstreet wrote seventy-seven meditations over the course of several years.

For all the prose she left behind, however, Anne Bradstreet is best known for her poetry. Anne's poetry has often been divided into two categories. First comes the *long* poems of heroic couplets, line after line of rhyme after rhyme. These poems comprise most of the collection in *The Tenth Muse*, and they are organized primarily by a series of "Quaternions" (the four elements, the four humors, the four ages of man, the four seasons of the year, and the four

[25] For the complete text of Leigh's treatise, see *Women's Writing in Stuart England: The Mothers' Legacies of Dorothy Leigh, Elizabeth Joscelin, and Elizabeth Richardson*, ed. Sylvia Brown (Phoenix Mill: Sutton Publishing, 1999), 3–87. In addition, see *Mother's Advice Books*, ed. Susan C. Staub, in *Printed Writings 1641–1700*, series II, part one, vol. 3 (Routledge, 2002). See also Jennifer Heller, *The Mother's Legacy in Early Modern England* (Routledge, 2011).

monarchies). Some additional elegies and formal verses fill out this category, usually interpreted as more "public" and usually assigned an earlier stage in Bradstreet's writing career—though both of these claims have been challenged in more recent scholarship.

Second comes the *shorter* poems: the "lyric" verse, the "domestic" poetry, such as love poems to her husband or elegies for her grandchildren. These verses were never put in print while she lived, and therefore they became known as more "private"—though again, *all* of her verse circulated in a similar manner among family and friends through manuscript. These poems move away from heroic couplets. Many of them, including a longer, rhapsodic nature poem called "Contemplations" (taken up by some of the poets in this collection), employ a seven-line stanza that rhymes ABABCCC. Those final three rhymes of each stanza create a sense of closure, and yet many of the poems do not close with pious finality, leading to the various traditions that have interpreted Anne Bradstreet as a rebel within the puritan cause. At any rate, when modern readers find themselves moved by a Bradstreet poem, it is almost always these shorter and potentially later verses, which anticipate more closely the historical trajectory of poetry as it moved from a previous era's interest in long, classical poems to the modern era's love of brief powerful lyrics.[26]

In their poetry, puritans (as well as most non-puritans of the period) seldom saw originality as desirable. Art did not aim at the novel or the innovative. Instead, it took inherited forms and mastered them, imitating to a new perfection. While Anne Bradstreet wrote all kinds of verse across her life and career, one standard narrative has suggested that she first attempted to imitate others before then mastering the art and expressing an original voice. No doubt Bradstreet developed as a poet. And it does seem clear that the poems we can date as later have a deeper tone and often a more intimate voice. Yet Bradstreet would never have valued originality as such. Instead, she found her way to such lyric verses while staying true to what she had always understood as the good and the beautiful.

The puritan sense of what counted as good and beautiful entailed a rejection of artistic ornamentation or anything baroque. Ornate language that drew attention to itself could easily slip into the sin of pride—a poet pointing at one's own work rather than using that work to point at God. As a result,

[26] On the development of the lyric as the dominant form of poetry, see Virginia Jackson, *Dickinson's Misery: A Theory of Lyric Reading* (Princeton: Princeton University Press, 2005).

puritan preachers and authors developed what has often been described as a "plain style," a way of speaking and writing that tried to make language transparent so that it could move readers with the spiritual realities that lay beyond. Reading, for puritans, aimed at a transformation of the self through an experience and recognition of the truth. Such a principle behind the act of reading guided the point and purpose of writing. When Anne Bradstreet describes her poetry as "homespun," therefore, she situates it within a tradition of modesty while also associating it with a lack of ornamentation, a plain style that suited puritan poetics well.[27]

In developing the plain style, however, the puritans never released their grip on the power of image, simile, and metaphor. Because the plain style achieved its power by reaching and touching the heart, it frequently pulled from all five senses and made reference to the material stuff of everyday life. Parallelism, repetition, amplification, and the usual devices of poetry (such as alliteration, enjambment, caesura, and rhyme) could all be turned to God's work of transforming lives and touching the heart with grace. Puritans had a particular art form, but it was no less artistic for all its insistence on being plain.[28]

But just how puritan *was* Anne Bradstreet? That question remains live for most readers of her work. Long ago, the biographer Josephine Piercy described her as "a Puritan woman who could not always accept the doctrine of her contemporaries" (preface). She was "capable of questioning and even of rebellion."[29] Part of this line assumes a puritanism focused on sin and damnation. As Piercy goes on to explain, "In none of [Bradstreet's] other writings do we smell the sulphurous fumes of Hell. We do not feel that hers was the avenging God of the Puritans."[30] That may be true—and certainly it constitutes part of her enduring appeal—but that absence of wrath does not necessarily mean she was any less puritan. Rather than using her loving tone and intimate concerns to move her out of puritanism, we might instead shift

[27] According to Deanna Fernie, Bradstreet's "term 'homespun' consciously sets her plain style, which she had employed in the private poems and elegies never intended for publication, against the riches of the Old World models on which she had based so much of her earlier verse" (28). Here we see the traditional narrative of an earlier and later Bradstreet, much-challenged now, but nonetheless Fernie makes an important point about differentiating Bradstreet's plain style from the very models on which she built. See Deanna Fernie, "The Difficult Homages of Berryman and Bradstreet," *Symbiosis* 7.1 (2003): 11–34.

[28] For a more extensive overview of Puritan literary genres and styles, see Abram Van Engen, "The Puritan Culture of Letters," in *A Companion to American Literature*, vol. 1, *Origins to 1820*, ed. Susan Belasco, Theresa Strouth Gaul, et al. (John Wiley and Sons, 2020), 51–72.

[29] Josephine Piercy, *Anne Bradstreet* (New York: Twayne, 1965).

[30] Ibid., 36.

our understanding of puritanism to allow for its inclusion of loving tones and intimate concerns. The puritans preached both damnation and salvation, both fear and comfort, both sin and grace—never the dark without the light. And they insisted throughout their days on the lovingkindness of God. Bradstreet's poetry picks up that strain, attempting to rest in the mercy and sovereignty of God, even (or especially) at moments of greatest hardship and tragedy.

Bradstreet may have been a rebel. She may have taken her own strain of puritanism further than most puritans would have been willing to go. She may have nursed many unanswered questions with a restless mind. She may have kicked against the confines of a theology too tightly drawn. Or she may have taken up elements all present within puritanism and pushed them to her own ends and means. She may not have been unique among puritans in doing so. Whatever she did, the puritans themselves seemed to think it fitting. They took her poetry to London and put it in print. They praised her as *The Tenth Muse Lately Sprung Up in America.* They cherished her writings and published even more of her poems following her death. They passed her manuscripts from one hand to another and preserved her works down to the present day. Now, almost four centuries after she lived, Anne Bradstreet represents a distinct voice from early New England and remains an important foundation of American poetry—a woman who became the first from North America to publish a book of poems, leaving a legacy still printed, still read, still resisted, and still inspiring new encounters even now.

The Poetic Response

The poets in this volume take up that legacy in multiple ways. Many sense the heft of what Bradstreet leaves out of her writing. They respond to the provocations of a historical fact: Bradstreet's poetry and prose is silent on some of the most pressing issues of her day. Bradstreet's writing never registers her impressions of the Indigenous people her settlements displaced or the Black Americans among whom she lived and whose labor and cultural achievements enabled her own. The poets in this collection bear down on these silences and erasures, highlighting what Kimberly L. Becker calls the "negative spaces" of her writing and providing critical complements to Bradstreet's poetic elisions. They attend to what Bradstreet does not say, what she perhaps did not see. They sense cultures, relationships, and environments she did not recognize or would not acknowledge. For Shane

McCrae, Bradstreet's poems evoke "[t]he chained Atlantic," although they never examine it. James Thomas Stevens puts Bradstreet into relationship with Indigenous women including Haudenosaunee mothers and grandmothers who recited poems for centuries before Bradstreet and her kin arrived in America. Unlike Bradstreet, as he writes, "Our women did not have to justify themselves or their time . . . Haudenosaunee women had the agency and freedom to spend the hours they needed to remember and recite, to ensure that future generations would know the proper wording of our ways." Bradstreet admired and imitated other poets, but Stevens's reading of Bradstreet points out her participation in a poetic tradition that preceded and exceeded her understanding. Kimberly Johnson voices this interest in the unplumbed reaches of Bradstreet's world when she concludes: "I claim the truest picture of the poet in what was, finally, left out."

The poets in this collection also see ways that Bradstreet's writings contain traces of meanings and vistas obscured by linguistic convention or the sheer volume of her literary output. Bradstreet's longest poems often exhaust the patience of her contemporary readers; they sometimes even exhausted her. "*My Subject's bare, my Brains are bad,/ Or better Lines you should have had*" she writes at the end of her long poem "The Four Seasons of the Year."[31] Our contributors, perhaps sympathetic to this sense of defeat, are willing to overlook Bradstreet's self-confessed failings and see moments of deftness and even brilliance in her weighty set of works. By directing our attention to the most dexterous and unexpected lines in Bradstreet's famously longwinded quaternions, Linda Gregerson makes a sensitive case that in these poems (often neglected by critics in favor of Bradstreet's shorter, personal poetry) the careful reader finds "Bradstreet at her most enchanting." Mary Jo Bang and Niki Herd make a version of Gregerson's interpretive practice into poetic process by stripping away sections of Bradstreet's poetry and prose to reveal striking, spare verse encrusted within Bradstreet's sometimes cumbersome writing. They illustrate the observation of Dan Beachy-Quick, who writes, "a poem can hold within itself many poems; a word can enfold within itself many words; and a syllable, so small a sound, is a wilderness entire." John Keene extracts a few of Bradstreet's most famous lines and creates a puzzle of them to showcase the possibility of "unearthing and revealing new meanings from her poems and newly created ones." The reconfigured or stripped-down versions of Bradstreet's poems hint at a surprisingly modern sensibility enfolded in her work—didacticism shot through with doubt.

[31] Bradstreet, *Poems and Meditations*, 105.

Little wonder, given how vulnerable Bradstreet made herself on the subjects of doubt, desire, and pain, that many poets in this volume find themselves seeking out her company. "Let's imagine Anne Bradstreet alongside me on this walk, and we talk a bit, and she adds a phrase or two between my stanzas," David Baker proposes. "My ghost companion." The result is a conversation that resonates across planes of existence. Even poets who foreground the considerable difference between their lives and Bradstreet's—such as Karen An-hwei Lee, whose aunties from Taiwan were baffled and unimpressed by puritan landmarks and artifacts in Massachusetts—find themselves relating to Bradstreet on personal terms. "I offer my own American narrative, so different from Bradstreet's, to point more honestly toward what we share: the condition of American women who write poems," Kathy Fagan writes. In much the way that Baker, Lee, and Fagan draw Bradstreet into the present, Rigoberto González, Cindy Veach, and Eduardo C. Corral write themselves into Bradstreet's world. González addresses Bradstreet in the voice of the New Spain poet and philosopher Sor Juana Inés de la Cruz, while Veach's poetic speaker addresses Bradstreet in the second person—imagining her as a young woman, and then a mother, and finally as a not-quite-departed soul. "Poetry was your tool to reach/ beyond the grave, pass down to us/ your story," the speaker recognizes. Corral's poem "Arbella" is written in Bradstreet's voice as she observes the celestial and the mundane lap against each other during her Atlantic crossing.

The pain attending Bradstreet's physical body repeatedly asserts itself in her own work and in the works in this collection—as in "Arbella," where the speaker imagines, "I'm back/ in an orchard. My neck/ needled by insects." Anne Myles feels keenly her distance from Bradstreet and her environment, yet she grants the transtemporal quality of the physical sensations they share. She writes, "That's the one thing I can be sure links us: what it feels like to exist inside a body." Bradstreet's body was tormented throughout her life. Both John Berryman and Eavan Boland imagine Bradstreet pockmarked by the smallpox she contracted as a young woman, although Margaret Olofson Thickstun notices that her brother-in-law remarks on her "comely face/ That in its native beauty has such grace" in his dedicatory poem in *The Tenth Muse*—"and if her face had been disfigured by scars, such a couplet would be egregious and cruel," she reasons.[32] But if Bradstreet was not disfigured by disease, she was certainly disabled. Daniel Borzutzky contemplates the

[32] Thickstun, "Introduction," 4.

"wasting pains" Bradstreet suffered throughout her life and Joanne Diaz acknowledges her rightful place within a "now well-recognized corpus of illness narratives that shed light on 'the kingdom of the sick.'" Puritan ministers regarded pain as another instrument wielded by a reforming God, but in representing her experience with sickness in poetic form, Bradstreet preserves versions of herself in illness and despair that talk back to the pious saint who emerges from fits of sickness healed and fortified. Since the nineteenth century, when her personal poetry was widely published, readers have been most drawn to these versions of Bradstreet—Bradstreet in pain, in doubt, in grief. Sophie Cabot Black and Marilyn Nelson imagine Bradstreet as if she were able to give voice to the full range of these emotions without disciplining them via literary or religious conventions into expressions of submission.

Readers of this collection will see Bradstreet's emotions, faith, culture, craft, and biography in new and sometimes unsettling lights through the prisms contemporary poets hold up to her work. The poems and essays gathered in this volume de-form and re-form Bradstreet's writing in ways that show what was always there—what she created and left behind—and what readers through the generations have added, and still add, to her poetic vision. Not all these poets laud or even commend Bradstreet, although some do, but Bradstreet did not expect to be adored. She asked only to be remembered. She wrote, she told her children, "that when I am no more with you, yet I may be daily in your remembrance."[33] This collection honors the spirit of that request and in doing so makes the same claim on its readers. Remember the poets of our generation, this book asks, and how they remembered the writing left to their care.

Although poetic labor is often perceived as a solitary art, poets always practice their art in conversation with others. They respond to the provocations of human experience, environments, other poets, readers anticipated or imagined, the divine, and even different versions of themselves. And they write to provoke responses. In assuring readers that his sister-in-law did not wish to appear in print, John Woodbridge makes a canny, qualified claim about the poet's aspirations for her work: "I have presumed to bring to public view what she resolved should never in such a manner see the Sun," he wrote in preface to the *Tenth Muse.* It may well be true that Bradstreet never wanted her poems brought to public view in *a printed collection.* But it does not follow

[33] Bradstreet, *Poems and Meditations,* 305.

that she wanted to hide her poems or keep them from reaching readers. As Woodbridge relates, many "scattered papers" containing Bradstreet's poems were already in circulation among "affected" readers when her manuscript arrived in London.[34] Throughout her writing, Bradstreet addresses kind readers as well as readers she expects will be unimpressed or alienated by her verse. She talks to God, to herself, and even to her poems. In responding to Bradstreet, the poets in this volume enter and extend a lively, ongoing conversation while expanding it to encompass a new generation of readers—each of us invited to discover how Bradstreet speaks to us and participate with our own response.

A Note on the Organization of This Collection

This collection presents and encourages new readings of Anne Bradstreet's work. We considered ordering the volume according to form, genre, or theme but felt each of those organizational schemes threatened to constrain and close off possible readings. Instead, we open the collection with an essay and a poem by Eavan Boland, both of which previously appeared elsewhere and inspired our vision for this project. Thereafter, we have arranged the works that follow alphabetically by the contributors' names. We hope this light editorial touch allows readers to see the diverse ways these poets relate to Bradstreet's poetry and prose, to each other, to other poets, and to generations of readers of Bradstreet and her contemporaries.

[34] Bradstreet, *Poems and Meditations*, 341.

Eavan Boland

Finding Anne Bradstreet

1

This is a piece about Anne Bradstreet. But there is another subject here as well. Its nature? For want of an exact definition, it is subject matter itself: that bridge of whispers and sighs over which one poet has to travel to reach another, out of which is formed the text and context of a predecessor. That journey into the past—not just Anne Bradstreet's but my own—is the substance of this essay.

I have always been fascinated by the way poets of one time construct the poets of a previous one. It can be an invisible act, arranged so that none of the awkwardly placed struts are visible. But the discussion of invisibility is not my intention. I am interested in the actual process of reconstruction, in the clear and unclear motives with which a poet from the present goes to find one from the past. I am interested, therefore, in the actions and choices that have the power to turn a canon into something less authoritarian and more enduring: from a set text into a living tradition. The sometimes elusive, yet utterly crucial, difference between a canon and a tradition is also part of this piece. So in that sense I want the plaster work to show and the background noise to be heard.

All of this seems worth saying at the beginning because I found Anne Bradstreet first in a revealing context. Not in her own words: not in the quick, fluent, and eventually radical cadences that mark her style. My first discovery of her had an ominous irony about it, so I will begin with that.

American poetry was hard to find in Dublin when I was a young poet. It was the mid-sixties. The names of American poets and their poems were not just unavailable in the bookshops: they were unavailable in the air. Part of that was simply enclosure. In the previous decades Ireland had come through an intense, inward adventure of its own. Its own poetry, its own poets, its domestic sense of having beaten the odds in both a historic and

Anne Bradstreet Now. Abram Van Engen and Mary Eyring, Oxford University Press.
 DOI: 10.1093/9780197811191.003.0001

aesthetic sense were the dominant tropes of its literary self-perception. In that sense, the Irish poetry world stood on what Arnold eloquently called "burning ground." Everyone shared in it. Everyone stood on it. It was an exciting literary culture, precisely because it was so enclosed. In a newspaper article, Patrick Kavanagh made a vivid distinction between literary provincialism and parochialism. Parochialism, he wrote, was that blind conviction of being at the center of things, of knowing no other place: it was the summer crossroads where he first made up ballads on football. It was the city that talked about itself endlessly: Joyce's city, with its draped curtains, glittering coastline, and malicious jokes. Provincialism, however, was the hankering for an elsewhere, an anxious measuring of the local against some other, distant standard. In that sense Dublin was—in the best sense—parochial.

A few things got through: a random sampling of the excitements of elsewhere. One of these was *Homage to Mistress Bradstreet* by John Berryman. Published in 1953 in the *Partisan Review*—and then as a volume in 1956—it was a tour de force, a cunning mixture of eulogy and elegy. Its language and syntax, its odd and vehement music had packed its energies in Yeats' proverbial ice and salt and readied them to cross the Atlantic. Over the next decade, the poem made its way into the conversations of young Irish poets. Some of this was because of Berryman himself. He came to Dublin in the mid-sixties, made friends, made enemies, caused a certain amount of mayhem, and briefly entered a poetic way of life that thrived on all three.

I remember struggling with *Homage to Mistress Bradstreet.* It was not easy to read for any student or young poet who was used to the Irish poem. It bore no resemblance to anything else. It was a rough, sinuous evocation of a snowy New England I had never seen, a Puritan rubric I had never heard of, a historical reinvention I knew next to nothing about. As a piece of information, it was a lot less clear than *Lycidas* and a lot less transparent than *Adonais.* It was also stubbornly mannered, hard to follow, given to cross-jumps of tone and point of view. I was twenty years old and a bad-tempered parochial in Kavanagh's definition, and I was not at all sure I wanted to persevere with it.

Yet my first information about Anne Bradstreet came from that poem. "Born 1612 Anne Dudley, married at 16 Simon Bradstreet, a Cambridgeman, steward to the Countess of Warwick & protégé of her father Thomas Dudley, secretary to the Earl of Lincoln. Crossed in the *Arbella*, 1630, under Governor Winthrop."[1] But none of those practical details arrested

[1] John Berryman, *Homage to Mistress Bradstreet and Other Poems* (New York: Noonday Press, 1968), 10.

me. The woman, the poet, was not yet visible. What disturbed and struck me were those fifty-seven stanzas. I didn't give them up. I continued to read. I floundered around in the richly divided identities of the piece. Part ode. Part dialogue. Part harangue. Part séance. And then the poet's voice, usurping the very identity he is seeking out.

(2)

Outside the New World winters in grand dark
white air lashing high thro' the virgin stands
foxes down foxholes sigh,
surely the English heart quails, stunned.
I doubt if Simon than this blast, that sea,
spares from his rigour for your poetry
more. We are on each other's hands
who care. Both of our worlds unhandled us. Lie stark,

(3)

thy eyes look to me mild. Out of maize & air
your body's made, and moves. I summon, see,
from the centuries it.
I think you won't stay. How do we
linger, diminished, in our lovers' air,
implausibly visible, to whom, a year,
years, over interims; or not;
to a long stranger; or not; shimmer and disappear.[2]

These stanzas by Berryman prove the point: using the materials of a different moment, he boldly and obstinately constructs a poet and a past. By the time the poem concludes, he has forced his way into the presence of Anne Bradstreet: that young woman who sailed from England at the age of eighteen, who found the Massachusetts winters harsher than those in Lincolnshire, who bore American children, who wrote love poems to her husband, who resolved her quest for style in a radical, domestic polemic. The problem is that by the time the poem is over, we know how the Massachusetts winter drifts down through a broken syntax, how a scalding faith may once have sounded, how musical those names and salutations were. We can even

[2] Ibid., 11.

guess about John Berryman's need for a past, a place, a source. But what do we know about her?

2

Anne Dudley was born in 1612, in Northamptonshire, in an England that had been nine years without its imperious queen and would, in another four, lose William Shakespeare and the raffish ethos of the Tudor world. Post-Elizabethan England. Already sowing the wind of the Civil War that was less than thirty years away. Already feeling the pinch and reproach of real-life Malvolios.

Her father was Thomas Dudley, at first clerk to Judge Nicolls in Northamptonshire and then steward of the earl of Lincoln's estate in Sempringham. These were not great people, but they lived in the shadow and peace of greatness. Her father would have known about fine wines and treasured books and the weighty ermines of the court. He would have talked to the ambitious builders and covetous architects of the period. Although he himself had never been to university, he had been tutored by a graduate, so he was able to give his daughter some knowledge of Greek and Latin and French.

It is hardly possible to imagine that England. It was a paradox, a contradiction, a place marching toward regicide and fratricide yet still in sight of the glories and upheavals of the Elizabethan Age. Although Anne Dudley must have heard reminiscences, within the shelter of the earl of Lincoln's estates, of the Armada, of the queen, of ships returning with silks and spices and new tastes and stolen riches, her reality was darker. When the Massachusetts Bay Company was formed in 1628, she was sixteen years old. Her father and her new husband, Simon Bradstreet, were founding members. The nonconformist protest was intensifying, and rage at the taxes and restrictions of Charles I was suddenly the text for action. The old England, with its grace, pride, and remembrance, was now a life-threatening fiction.

In 1630 these founding members began their "errand into the wilderness," as Samuel Danforth called it.[3] The *Arbella* set sail from Southampton. Three

[3] Samuel Danforth, "Brief Recognition of New England's Errand into the Wilderness," in *American Sermons: The Pilgrims to Martin Luther King Jr.*, ed. Michael Warner (New York: Library of America, 1999), 151.

months later John Winthrop wrote that "there came a smell off the shore like the smell of a garden."[4] They were safe. They landed at Massachusetts. For Puritanism it was a new context. For America a new history. For Anne Bradstreet a new story. Or half of one. As she steps onto the shore of New England, she disappears. The young woman who loved England is lost in America. "I . . . came into this country, where I found a new world and new manners, at which my heart rose."[5]

Anne Bradstreet is that rare thing: a poet who is inseparable from history. The proportions are not usually so equal and compelling. She can be located in the same way as a place name on a map, and we can judge the distance more accurately because of that. After all, it was history that swept her up, out of the graceful houses and prospects of Lincolnshire and into a three-month sea voyage. History that brought her to the shores of Massachusetts. History that included her in the rigorous self-definition of the Puritans. History that almost demoted her to a figure in the background of a turbulent time.

But when she encountered the New World, she was met not so much by history as by daily routine and hardship. The first winter was cruel and hungry. Food was scarce. "Clams, and muscles [*sic*], and ground-nuts and acorns"[6] must have seemed a poor diet after the feasts of Lincolnshire. Even her father wrote the bleak truth back to England: "There is not a house where is not one dead, and some houses many."[7] But her life at that moment was set in a mold of survival and compliance, both. First the hard winters, the forced adaptation. Then it was swift and relentless shifting: from Salem to Charlestown, to Cambridge, to Ipswich, and finally to Andover. With each move, each unquestioning pursuit of her husband and father, each trekking after Dudley and Simon Bradstreet, she wrote herself deeper into that difficult history.

The mid-thirties found the Dudleys and Bradstreets living in Ipswich, with a parcel of land, some more prosperity, a gradual easing of conditions. Now twenty-four years old, with two children, Anne Bradstreet had partially recovered from the lameness she had suffered during her eighteenth year. She was raising her children, absorbing her landscape, writing in earnest.

[4] John Winthrop, "Journal," in *Winthrop Papers*, 5 vols. (Boston: Massachusetts Historical Society, 1929–47), 2:259.

[5] *The Works of Anne Bradstreet in Prose and Verse*, ed. John Harvard Ellis (Charlestown, MA: A. E. Cutter, 1867), 5.

[6] Alexander Young, *Chronicles of the First Planters* (Boston: Little, Brown, 1846), 381.

[7] Thomas Dudley, "Letter to Countess of Lincoln," in ibid., 325.

And there I leave her for the moment so as to widen the story of which she is a part.

3

The mysterious life and achievement of Anne Bradstreet—her occasionally surprising and quick-moving poems, her fresh and intense outlook—is a story I will keep circling around here. No one approach is completely satisfactory. History, culture, political change are all part of it. But not all of it. Some of her truth may have less to do with history than with social anachronism. Because Anne Bradstreet is a founding American poet, it is easy to forget that she was also a dying star in the context of European poetry: a poet writing against a background of adamant faith from a country deeply troubled by the usurpation of religion by politics. A poet of the coteries, when the wider community was becoming fashionable. A poet whose inner and outer life remained powerfully undivided, when the subtle divisions between them—from which romanticism would eventually emerge—was beginning to evolve in England.

It is ironic that had Anne Bradstreet stayed in England, her ecosystem would have been radically different. In a country with an incipient Civil War, a poisoned and politicized religious system, and, after that, an approaching Restoration, where women would be considered bait for princes rather than poets in their own right, how would she have fared? Any consideration of Anne Bradstreet's work has to take this into account: she left a poetic tradition in which she would almost certainly have remained anonymous and founded another in which she is visible, anomalous, and crucial.

4

How do I see Anne Bradstreet? The answer is not simple. To start with, there is no figure in Irish poetry like her. To read of her travels and her pieties, to consider the male power that surrounded her and to which she deferred, and finally to hear her plain-spoken and resistant voice convince me of some out-of-the-way truths. Here is one of them:

When we speak of the way a poet constructs the poets of another age—which is a good deal of my subject—certain things get missed. When I was a young poet, it was an article of faith that modernism was the watershed, the event that changed every poet's view of the recent and distant past. If I wasn't persuaded then, I am even less convinced now.

No, the real watershed—the place where poets divide—is in the version of those centuries—the sixteenth, seventeenth, and eighteenth—which are talismanic possessions for the young poet. Not just in poetry. After all, in those centuries galaxies were found and poetic forms rediscovered; faiths were changed and diseases named. Those are the centuries that divide or attach poets.

Those are the last continents of time where the hinterland of poetry lay as a gleaming, shining distance, still to be named and changed. Just to see that hinterland, just to lay claim to those possessions, is for the young poet often the first unforgettable sensing of the freedom and the grandeur of the art.

But my version of those centuries is the Irish, not the British or American one. There is a world of difference. As Anne Bradstreet was seeking the New World, Ireland was losing the old one. As the Massachusetts Bay Colony was testing its ideas of grace, Ireland was sinking deeper into its knowledge of abandonment. As Simon Bradstreet was touching the light of manifest destiny, the Gaelic order, the bards and the unlucky princes of Ireland were preparing to learn the opposite. And what Anne Bradstreet took with her into her poetry, into the New World—that upward roll of Elizabethan music—is the very cadence that poisoned the wells for the Irish poets.

So when I picture her, this figure from the time and language that dispossessed my own, how can I see her clearly? I am not John Berryman, imagining her on the deck of the *Arbella*, founding his tradition, guaranteeing his music, fearing her elusiveness—"I think you won't stay."[8] Unlike Berryman, my syntax was guaranteed by another group of poets.

But the truth is, I do see her. And somehow the fact that I do, despite not counting her century into my inheritance, seems to prove my point: that the reconstruction of the past, the reconstruction of poet by poet, is willful, inventive, compulsive. The truth is, I cannot afford not to see Anne Bradstreet. She lays her claim across every boundary, in spite of every distance. What's more, she tests my own powers of reconstruction. Pock-marked, slightly lame, outspoken and astonishing in her ability to survive the odds, she comes before me.

[8] "Homage to Mistress Bradstreet" (line 40), in Berryman, *Homage to Mistress Bradstreet.*

5

Anne Bradstreet was thirty-eight when her poetry was published. Not in her native Massachusetts, not even in America, but in an England she would never see again. Her brother-in-law arranged it. He returned to England in 1650, bringing a manuscript of her poems with him and arranging for its publication as *The Tenth Muse, Lately Sprung Up in America*. It would appear to be a strange route to publication but only if seen through modern eyes. Publication for contemporary poets has been a single and sometimes superstitious act: the first book, then the second. But I suspect that in Puritan Massachusetts, as once in eighteenth-century Ireland, the line between what was broadcast and published and locally known and communally written was not at all as clear as it became later: that there was a rich, blurred run of colors at the edge of private authorship and public faith.

The Tenth Muse was published through the efforts of her brother-in-law, the Reverend John Woodbridge, who wrote a winning and eloquent "Epistle to the Reader" at the start of the book. It is Anne Bradstreet's only publication in her lifetime. Not until she had been dead six years did a second, amended edition of *The Tenth Muse* come out. A third followed in 1758. This is a leisurely publication schedule by any standards, and not until 1867 did John Harvard Ellis produce a scholarly and complete text of this book, with more authoritative inclusions.

In his "Epistle to the Reader" Woodbridge is quick to disclaim any poetic vanity on the part of his sister-in-law. He remarks that he has "presumed to bring to publick view what she [Bradstreet] resolved should in such manner never see the sun."[9] Despite this, the poems are only partially successful. A heavy Spenserian shadow hangs over them, as if her girlhood ghost were haunting the paneled rooms of Sempringham. They pay elaborate and conventional tribute to the old heroes and graces of her past: Philip Sidney; her father, Thomas Dudley. The public tone often falters; the language rarely shines. Only *In Honour of That High and Mighty Princess Queen Elizabeth of Happy Memory* cracks open to suggest strength and craft. Despite a clumsy percussion, despite the rhymes swerving and chasing the sentiments around the page, there is a vigor of nostalgia, something haunting and striking about this memory of a powerful woman, written by a woman just learning her own power:

[9] Quoted in Ellis, *Works*, 84.

Who was so good, so just, so learn'd, so wise,
From all the kings on earth she won the prize.
Nor say I more than duly is her due,
Millions will testify that this is true.
She hath wiped off th' aspersion of her sex,
That women wisdom lack to play the rex.
Spain's monarch, says not so, nor yet his host;
She taught them better manners, to their cost.[10]

There is no mystery about *The Tenth Muse*. It is the oddly confident, sometimes accomplished work of a well-born woman. The mystery comes later. After 1653, in the years following the death of her father, Anne Bradstreet's poems changed. The subjects closed in. Her feelings, her children, the life of her home, the spirit of her marriage—these, rather than elegies for lost courtiers, became her themes. The music shifted: the volume was turned down; the voice became at once more private and more intense. A quick-walking cadence accompanied the neighborly, definite voice in which she now told her story. These were cadences that came from the New England moment in which she lived. At last, the complicated England of her youth was receding.

To My Dear and Loving Husband
If ever two were one, then surely we
If ever man were loved by wife, then thee;
If ever wife was happy in a man,
Compare with me, ye women, if you can.
I prize thy love more than whole mines of gold
Or all the riches that the East doth hold.
My love is such that rivers cannot quench,
Nor ought but love from thee, give recompense.
Thy love is such I can no way repay,
The heavens reward thee manifold, I pray.
Then while we live, in love let's so persevere
That when we live no more, we may live ever.
(225)

[10] *The Works of Anne Bradstreet*, ed. Jeannine Hensley, with a foreword by Adrienne Rich (Cambridge, MA: Harvard University Press, 1967), 195–98. All verse quotations are from this volume. Subsequent pagination will be indicated parenthetically in the essay proper.

Or this, from the last year of her life:

In Reference to Her Children, 23 June 1659
I had eight birds hatched in one nest,
Four cocks there were, and hens the rest.
I nursed them up with pain and care,
Nor cost, nor labour did I spare,
Till at the last they felt their wing,
Mounted the trees, and learned to sing;
Chief of the brood then took his flight
To regions far and left me quite.
My mournful chirps I after send,
Till he return, or I do end:
Leave not thy nest, thy dam and sire,
Fly back and sing amidst this choir.
(232–234)

Where does this voice come from? On the surface, it seems to be earned and made by a woman caught in an unusually rich and powerful dialogue with an authoritarian tradition. Whatever name is given to that authority—maleness, Puritanism, doctrine—the dialogue is sweetened by a strange irony. It appears that the Puritan world can offer a woman poet more permission for domestic and ordinary detail than the Elizabethan one ever did. This is not to diminish the authorship. It is Anne Bradstreet's unique achievement that she could burrow into the cracks, discover the air of history, and find a breathing space to be Puritan, poet, and woman:

I washed thy face, but more defects I saw,
And rubbing off a spot still made a flaw.
I stretched thy joints to make thee even feet,
Yet still thou run'st more hobbling than is meet;
In better dress to trim thee was my mind,
But nought save homespun cloth i' th' house I find.
("The Author to Her Book," 221)

As Adrienne Rich wrote of her: "The web of her sensibility stretches almost invisibly within the framework of Puritan literary convention; its texture is essentially both Puritan and feminine."[11] And the Puritan spirit is more easily reconciled, it seems, within the domestic parameter, with the willful, personal intention of the earthly artist, envious of being remembered. "You once desired me," she writes to her son in 1664, "to leave something for you in writing that you might look upon, when you should see me no more."[12]

In the final years of the 1660s, when a lavish court has been reinstated in the country of her birth, Anne Bradstreet—only a few years from her death in 1672—is a world away from power and costume. She has become the author of a bold, personal narrative, mourning her grandchildren, stripping out the rhythms she once learned as ornament, making them serve true feeling:

> I knew she was but as a withering flower,
> That's here today, perhaps gone in an hour;
> Like as a bubble, or the brittle glass,
> Or like a shadow turning as it was.
> ("In Memory of My Dear Grandchild Anne Bradstreet," 236)

But where did she get the permission for this? Did she really find the sustenance in a Puritan world for what looks remarkably like private and willful expression? The answer (or answers) to that question puts the most strain on the second subject of this piece: the relation between the past and present of poetry. Between the dead and living poet.

6

Anne Bradstreet not only lived in another time; she continues to dwell in a past that I could never hope to find. Strong-willed, displaced, she appears and disappears in front of me. The pock-marked young English girl, scarred by a mystery illness, becomes an American woman poet in the midst of a drama of fervor and faith, becomes the wife and daughter of powerful men, becomes mother of a powerful son to whom she confided her language and purpose.

[11] Hensley, *Works of Anne Bradstreet*, xix.
[12] Quoted in Hensley, *Works of Anne Bradstreet*, 271.

I wish I could see her clearly. I wish I could see the pen she wrote with. I wish I could reach back to those first hurt conversations in the Massachusetts colony, to her struggles with grace and her conflict with obedience. I wish I could see her in the house in Ipswich, with her children around her. "Nor cost, nor labour did I spare."[13]

The fact is, I can't. And to overlook this simple realization may well corrupt that contact between poet and poet that I began by considering. Poets of the present may invent the poets of the past all too easily, may wrench them from the disciplines and decisions of the world they lived in with such care and pain and disfigure them in a more convenient present.

The example of Anne Bradstreet is a sobering, chastening warning to such canon making. I cannot, as I've said, reconstruct her. If the young woman is unavailable, the older one is elusive. But even the poet that she is resists, in some strange way, any easy re-evaluation by the present. In this may lie one of the enduring fascinations of her work. So in summary I will try to outline some of that resistance here.

The challenge offered by Anne Bradstreet's work is partly to do with its time and location: its origins in one world and its outcome in another. But there is more to the issue than that. In a real way her work lays bare the possible corruptions of the invention of one poet by another, of the past by the present.

If one poet returned to another with simply the prejudices of a time, it would be awkward but understandable: there might be a risk of simplification but not erasure. But this is never the case. We return as poets to the past lugging the huge wing-beams and magical engines and turbines of our age. We drag them across subtleties and differences and demand that our predecessors learn to fly as we have. Providing, of course, they use our machines to do so.

Consider Anne Bradstreet. She lived in a community and adventure of faith, at a real and figurative distance from a continent where both were fading. She struggled with the very concepts of grace, unreason, and compliance that Europe was preparing to throw over. Her first poems—those in *The Tenth Muse*—were structured, formal, and derivative. Her final ones were sharp and musical and impossible to overlook. She waits to be reconsidered. But how can it be done?

[13] From "In Reference to Her Children, 23 June 1659," in Hensley, *Works of Anne Bradstreet*, 232.

In one sense she is a compelling figure precisely because she stands outside the categories we have prepared for the dialogue between past and present. Our concepts of what constitutes the public and private poem will not do when we approach her. Above all, our postromantic definition of what is the inner life and what the outer in poetry, and who patrols the borders, will not serve in her case. If we use these categories, we will blur the astringent angles of what she achieved. But how to do otherwise?

A quick look shows how. If we return to Anne Bradstreet with our definitions of the public and private poem and notions of nineteenth-century inner life, we will be drawn to a single and deceptive conclusion: the poems in *The Tenth Muse* are more wooden and fixed than Bradstreet's later poems. The later poems are fresh, warm, particular. How tempting it is to use our everyday categories of criticism to argue that her inner mind was freed by the death of her father; that this new freedom compelled her to negotiate the inner world of love and domesticity into a private poetry rather than an official one; that she found a private voice within the public ethos of Puritanism; that, if the truth were told, she is a subversive within the larger structures of the early American experience. These are certainly appealing propositions. But are they true?

It would be convenient if they were. It would make Anne Bradstreet immediately available to the poetic wisdoms of our own time. But I am not sure. As an Irish poet I see a flaw in those divisions between private and public. As a woman poet, I see a founding inaccuracy in this blueprint of the inner life. No, to understand her at all requires a break with the norms of psychobiography—far too often employed on poets and especially women poets—and an attempt to track her in the broader context where her works belong.

It is tempting to see the girl who left England in 1628 as young and singular, almost a child bride about to travel from ease to hardship, and to read back from her poetry to catalogue her adjustments and realizations. But this view is incomplete. No individual journey can explain the woman who suddenly, in 1662, could write with spirit, with a compelling contemporary eloquence, about desire in marriage, the death of children, the burning of her house. Another explanation is necessary.

The tense and elaborate world of poetry she left behind must have seemed a faraway dream in the mid-seventeenth century on the salty coasts of New England. But her shedding of that world is not easily measurable today. It would be a mistake to look for it in one act of style or one suppression of rhetoric. It has to be judged, like a quark or quasar, by absences, negations, negative energies, suppositions of space and distance.

The England that Anne Bradstreet left behind had already assigned a place to the poet. And it is clearly identified in those poems in *The Tenth Muse* in which she herself echoes the place-making energies of that canon. The place is not to be found in style. It is a series of angles and distances, a series of inferences by which poets reveal the ground they stand on by the words they choose.

By the time Anne Bradstreet sailed for America, the English poet had in these angles and relations an inner and outer world. Like a child, that poetic world had dissociated itself out of self-protection: it had split apart the better to handle the raw, intimate relation to power that history and society had ordained for the English poet of that time. The outer world was often coded into decorums, ornaments, pieces of rhetoric. The inner world was dark, raw, nihilistic. And this dichotomy reflected the fact that the poet of Elizabethan England, and before that Tudor England, was often an artist of grace and gifts who had learned the hard way—Surrey is an obvious example—that power offered no exemption, that poets must write in the shadow of the gallows, as well as in the light of favor. Above all, they had learned how to arm themselves with the gorgeous pastoral of prothalamion—the rivers, the nymphs, the musical harmonies—the better to infer a world of exclusion and pain.

What happened to Anne Bradstreet? To put it another way, What did not happen to her? She did not learn from the young Milton, the young Marvell. She did not see how ornament might imply disorder. She did not learn that the poet's place is in a split-apart world. In fact, the opposite. She came to enact in her life and her work a world of action, faith, expression, family, and ordinary adventure. And in the process the fissure healed. And suddenly—of course not suddenly—we have a woman in middle life whose children are gone, whose house has burned down, who makes no angles, distances, or perspective among faith, event, and feeling. They are all one. They have all happened. So she generates a poem in which they are indivisible, from a sensibility that is not divided. And she changes the history of poetry.

By this interpretation, Anne Bradstreet wrote—in her best and later work—in a community so scalded by change and history that the public and private were fused into one and the same. This is a rare circumstance for poetry. Nevertheless, I suspect her poems were indeed written in the crucible of that fusion: they document a privacy that was public and a public faith that was privately realized. They also presume the most intimate and exacting audience: one anxious to hear and see its own new adventures. If all this is true, then the later shift into the intimacy of poems about her husband, her children, her domestic life is not truly disruptive. The poems are merely continuations of this powerful intimacy between poet and community caught in the same dialogue of faith, duty, and reflection. Anne Bradstreet's poems shift and reassemble and shimmer with the hard-won confidence of that complex historical self. They are excitingly innocent of the sense that this is, by some definition of her own past, a smaller life. Most important, by being innocent of these definitions, she questions our own.

It would be wrong to make extravagant claims for Anne Bradstreet. Her work is memorable and strange and moving but also uneven and unrealized in certain parts. Yet it would also be wrong to deny how strongly she challenges our rights over the past. However powerful the relation between poet and poet, it must always yield to a poet like Anne Bradstreet, a poet whose work comes from a world both made and suffered and not at all ready to be erased by our easy assumptions, a poet who makes it clear that any relation with her must be on her terms also.

Originally published in *Green Thoughts, Green Shades: Essays by Contemporary Poets on the Early Modern Lyric*, edited by Jonathan F.S. Post, University of California Press, 2002, 176–190. Reprinted with permission.

Becoming Anne Bradstreet

It happens again
As soon as I take down her book and open it.

I turn the page.
My skies rise higher and hang younger stars.

The ship's rail freezes.
Mare Hibernicum leads to Anne Bradstreet's coast.

A blackbird leaves her pine trees
And lands in my spruce trees.

I open my door on a Dublin street.
Her child/her words are staring up at me:

In better dress to trim thee was my mind,
But nought save home-spun cloth, i' th' house I find.

We say *home truths*
Because her words can be at home anywhere—

At the source, at the end and whenever
The book lies open and I am again

An Irish poet watching an English woman
Become an American poet.

Originally published in *Shakespeare's Sisters: Women Writers Bridge Five Centuries*, Folger Shakespeare Library, 2012. Reprinted with permission.

David Baker

Six Meditations on a Poem

I'm walking across the shiny black asphalt of our local grocery parking lot. It's 7 a.m., straight up and down, and there are only a couple of cars, one pickup, no one else around. The store opens at 7 and I'm out of milk. It's also the end of May. The morning air hangs already humid, very still, yet several dozen of the seeds I love come floating—down, sideways, even back upward—out from the trees, out of the gray-blue sky, across the parking lot. They mark the season as well as any calendar. It's the cottonwoods. They grow in my village, Granville, Ohio, down along Raccoon Creek running alongside the grocery store; they grow through the low wetlands in and out of town and far beyond. Now you are—

> Crossing against traffic, an otherwise.
> Or the barest new breeze, slipping over
> the white barn,
>   itself a conditional—
>
> *Speak what they will—*

Anne Bradstreet Now. Abram Van Engen and Mary Eyring, Oxford University Press.
 DOI: 10.1093/9780197811191.003.0002

The cottonwood tree grows tall and can reach 100 feet in maturity. Its eastern variety (*populus deltoides*) is common across eastern North American and southeastern Canada. Its bark is silver-white and relatively smooth, though as they age the trees turn more fissured, darkening with the years. I love their big leaves, relatively late to come on and early in autumn to fall, and especially I love the magic of their catkin flowers that release seed-capsules (samaras) to split open, broadcasting all these tiny cottony billows, silky white, and seemingly weightless. One tree, according to my tree book, can produce 40 million seeds in a single season.

Is it a barn. Is it white. Either way
you pause, in a stillness, and the quick
thermal stalls.
                    But on they come, floating—

they are but wind—

I've been reading Anne Bradstreet again, the steady sanity of her poems, the balance of her language and form, the clarity of her tender but righteous worldview. Cottonwoods would have been plentiful in her Massachusetts villages, in Cambridge, Ipswich, and her eventual residence in Andover. I bet she'd have called the cottonwoods "stately," though I find no reference to the species in her writings. But she did refer to tall elms and oaks alike as "stately." In "Contemplations" she meditated on trees, on "goodly" rivers and "gliding streams," often drawn to these landscapes for the serenity and privacy they provided for her.

With their hundred hair-fine small fires.
Their bright filaments. Is this the city.
Each doorway, an exit,
                    a lit exhaustion—

In grass, on trees, in flight—

Mistress Bradstreet liked to walk. So do I. Roger Gilbert has a wonderful book, *Walks in the World,* about poetry, about poets walking, and the physical and meditative effect of just going on a walk. Wallace Stevens' great poem "An Ordinary Evening in New Haven," Wordsworth's masterpiece *The Prelude*, and so many more lyric poems take the occasion of the walk as a time to think and sing. Gilbert offers a typological sorting even the Puritans might appreciate. He says there are three distinct transformational effects that modern poets attain through the habit of walking: the cognitive, the meditation, and the aesthetic.

Where a soul weighs less than the word for it.
Between her last touch, the wings of it,
and a next stitch of breeze.
                                        They fill the air—

Some fall down. Some fly up—

But let's not get too analytical yet. "Now You Are" can be simply a poem about walking and spring—the week or two when milkweed silks fill the air, whether you're in the city or the country, whether there is a wind or stillness. Let's imagine Anne Bradstreet alongside me on this walk, and we talk a bit, and she adds a phrase or two between my stanzas. My ghost companion. The italic fragments are from her work, the poem "The Four Elements" and her letter "For My Dear Son Simon Bradstreet." I'm looking for all kinds of crossings-over—the street, the seeds in the air, our crosstalk, the centuries touching and dissolving. "The Four Elements" is beautiful for its passages on air and wind and on water. Those elegant, rhymed couplets of hers may be a ghost form for my poem, and her habit of reading God's large purposes into every single tiny natural thing plays across the background. I see all these floating cottonwood seeds as words, too, or Bradstreet angels, bits of a soul, glimpses of the many worlds.

And illuminate the air. Like a trembling
of waters where cottonwoods grow tall.
The cilia, the silk of them.
                                        Nothing's moving—

which may reveal a mind—

I think we live in many times at once, and we live in many places at once. Our words are hardly ours, as much as the gifts and intimations of all their previous uses. The meditative walk of my poem is looking for ways to find forms and voices of the plural, the ongoing, the here-and-now and just-beyond. Can a poem—fixed on the two-dimensional plane of a page—suggest third and further dimensions? Can a word or a phrase find its usages in more than a single sentence, in more than one person's voice? What are those magical silky seeds but answers of "yes" to the questions? They are ghosts, gifts, whispers, defying gravity, place, and time.

> When everything's on the move. Your soul is
> not just for other worlds—it's for this one.
> Like *something I leave*
>
> *for you in writing.*

Mary Jo Bang

The Flesh and the Spirit

[I was happy once] . . .once
I stood [&] heard two sisters:
past and things to come.

Art [is] industry [plus]
Substance: trophies
to wearing time—pearls and

eyes, or hands, only
in [the] mind. I do love, I do.
I do live, I do.

My thoughts reach at things
beyond what is. Angels
are porters there.

The streets transparent, the
waters pure. This is—if—
I take the world and all that.

Contemplations
The more I look[e]d, the more I grew
to wonder who gave light to skies. Being
fancy, Adam fancie[d] the apple: the
father of lyes. We are perpetual night,
the heavens and the earth (old) green,
stones, trees, winter, spring. Strength,
wisdom, oblivion. When I thought [of
how] trees excel, if the sun would shine,

Anne Bradstreet Now. Abram Van Engen and Mary Eyring, Oxford University Press.
 DOI: 10.1093/9780197811191.003.0003

there I['d] dwell. While on the ocean
I arrive at unknown coasts. So, Nature:
the spacious sea-green field. Each
pretty instrument long[s] for translation.
Draws curtains over names, ports,
pomp: all laid in rust when all are gone.

In the early 1990s, on a trip to or from somewhere, I found a hardcover first edition of a 1959 Faber & Faber book (dust jacket intact) in a used bookstore located in the Minneapolis airport: *Homage to Mistress Bradstreet and Other Poems* by John Berryman. I must have paid $12.00 for it, since that's the price lightly penciled above an inscription that reads, "To Mother for Birthday 1967 George." When George gave the book to his mother "for Birthday," Berryman was still alive. After a turbulent life, he jumped to his death from the Washington Avenue Bridge in Minneapolis on January 7, 1972.

The long poem didn't initially interest me. I much preferred Berryman's *77 Dream Songs*—reading that book had forever changed my idea of what a poem could be: a voice, *as if* one's own. I didn't understand then that *Homage to Mistress Bradstreet* was, in fact, also a type of "dream song," one in which Berryman and his idea of Bradstreet became a seamlessly interwoven voice that was sometimes *as if* it were hers, and other times, within the same line, *as if* it were his: "Women sleep sound. I was happy once . . / Something keeps on not happening, I shrink?)" (10.4–5)

I must have taken the book with me to a residency in Switzerland in 1999 because the essence of one of these lines from *Homage to AB* (23.5–8)—

> Sam, your uncle has had to
> go fróm us to live with God. 'Then Aunt went too?'
> Dear, she does wait still.
> Stricken: 'Oh. Then he takes us one by one.' My dear.

—found its way into a poem I wrote after seeing a partial solar eclipse on August 11 ("Eclipsed"):

> Specters they would be
> rooted eighty-two years in the same spot waiting
> for another and then an offhand remark and one by one
> (which is the way death takes us, he said)
> they took their shadows
> and went out of the garden and into the house.

Looking back, I find it rather odd that in spite of having lived with the ghost of Anne Bradstreet for some thirty years, I had never read a poem by her until this recent invitation to write "on any aspect of Anne Bradstreet's life, work, or world."

I began by rereading Berryman's *Homage to AB*, and then I read Bradstreet's poems. It occurred to me that one way to better understand how she was using language was to do an erasure of one of her long poems. That would allow me to isolate whatever I found most resonant. I chose "The Flesh and the Spirit," partly because the poem was long enough, but also because I was interested in the concepts of "flesh" and "spirit"—in what they may have meant to her, a seventeenth-century Puritan, and what they might mean to me, a twenty-first–century atheist with an interest in neuroscience.

From the first four lines of the poem—

In secret place where once I stood
Close by the Banks of Lacrim flood,
I heard two sisters reason on
Things that are past and things to come.

—I kept only "once I stood," "heard two sisters," and "past and things to come." While I admired the way Bradstreet metaphorized feeling "near [secret] tears" by placing the speaker close to the banks of a flooding river named Lacrim (from the Latin *lacrime*, "tears"), the language was too cryptic for my purposes. I added a bracketed ampersand (common in her time) to link the first two phrases, and used a colon to turn the "two sisters" into the parallel abstractions "the past" and the future, or, as she has it, "things to come."

What was missing, to my mind, was the sorrow that the second line conveyed, if one understood the work it was meant to do. I needed a substitute for that moment but one that would preserve the indirection of Bradstreet's inventive "Close by the Banks of Lacrim flood." I looked back at Berryman's *Homage* and found "I was happy once . . ." Not only would that bring Berryman into the poem—where surely he belonged—but it would bring the pathos, since "I was happy once . ." is heart breaking. The fact that Berryman's "once" echoed Bradstreet's "once" make the inclusion feel all the more fated. Plus, breaking the line after the second "once," allowed the repetition to feel emphatic (I was happy once . . . once," which heightened the sense of sorrow.

[I was happy once]. . .once
I stood [&] heard two sisters:
past and things to come.

I used the same methodology for the erasure of Bradstreet's "Contemplations" that I had used for "The Flesh and the Spirit," but with this second poem, I didn't find words I wanted to adopt until the fourth stanza (4.3–6):

The more I look'd, the more I grew [redacted]
[redacted] to [redacted]
[redacted] wonder [redacted]

And then, not again until 7.6 and 8.3.

7
[redacted]
Who gave [redacted] bright [redacted]

8
[redacted] to [redacted] Skies [redacted]

I lower cased the "S" in skies and modernized the "look'd" by adding a bracketed e: "look[e]d." I wouldn't have had to bracket the e, but I wanted to preserve the edges of where I had altered Bradstreet's language. It felt honest and respectful. Throughout both poems, I wanted the reader to see Bradstreet's words and my remodeling and to read into that coupling an alliance between two women writing four hundred years apart, in two very different worlds, each wondering about the fragility of life and the stamina required to write it.

Dan Beachy-Quick

Blessed Bee, Deerest Dear

(A dozen dozens for Anne Bradstreet)

Woo and woe rhyme. As do doe &
do. Doe you take this man to bee?
I doe. He woed me. So I wed him.
The hartless hind wants her deer
one. Whenever is two not two true?
Dove all alone is the past tense
of dive—a dove in the dark woods
into which I flew. I dove. Rhymes
with love. I've lived alone in the hive.
Cooed the & co. Love's etcetera. I
did, I died. Lay, lied. Bid the grammar
bee a bed, swallowed the wife, the why.

Anne Bradstreet Now. Abram Van Engen and Mary Eyring, Oxford University Press.
 DOI: 10.1093/9780197811191.003.0004

The heartless mind wants her dear
one, her bee, her once had been and so will
be, unto death, unto dearth, a spark
wood would woo turns to dust, you bee
my earth. Ere the air, another form of here
the doe do hear a song sing soft in her
soft ear. A word is many woods, many
woulds. Many woe before they woo &
saying I *doo* know not what they no nor
do. Father was a righteous man of hum.
Of humble words. Spelt aright the grain
wins winter o'er again. Agrain. A kind of

wooing, kin to woeing. Who knows who
is it it is they are? A mother's mouth
a moth flies out, child, child, there is
the moth, the month, the moon woos—
mouth the moon woods, such woe,
such mystery to wed, such cold fire
in which to write epitaphs. God is good
when God is goad. Adagio or a door. Adore
or go. I went, I goed. Time's so quick it's slow.
Whenever is one not one alone? A mother is
a minor form of mute before the all-mighty
All. A kind of alas that outlasts always—

praise, paradise. God grammars what's good
into plumbs and apples that thoroughly ripe
completely fall. The angels angle
Eden into other flames than swords—
turkey quills, turnkey wills, I would, I wood,
I wooed. A bed is ashes waiting to be,
& what is is what bees. I like to teach
the children to speak. I like their *A*
Bee Sees. A little death hides in the nest.
In the hive. I've lost so much I cannot say
how the poems say what they doe. Speak
the words I cannot say, an alphabet in the

wilderment, & ears mean many things more
than listening deerly to any sound
in the dark wood, years the doe so often
sighs. An ear of grain. An ear of again—
mute-of-cry. The children's children doe
die. The woulds wait their flame allmost
preordained. Time's so slow it's quick.
God's there in the needle's prick.
You get a cough and worry you've dyed
the wool the wrong color. The plum's
deep purple. Is it faith? Is it doubt?
Orange yolk of the hen's egg. Nothing rhymes

with no-thing. The poet loves her esses
hiding in the grass of her yesses.
& so I leave these poems behind that
here you may find what was liveing in
your mother's mind. Eternity doesn't
breathe, it bees. Doesn't sing, it stings.
What be the bee brought. Don't ask
me how I no. I just no. I know I doe—
the tree is a tree of the knowledge of—
memory. The apple blossom's yellow
pollen. I hived heaven in a honey cell sweet
as the muzzle of a dear. There are snakes

but there is no hell. A faithfull mouth
speaks prayses, Worldlings, even sorrow
is praise. A thankfull mouth clatters
vanities against mercy and asks where
the Judges bee. The child
holds to her ear the sea
shell and asks where the Judges bee—
is it, is it, mother doe tell, waves
in the nacre, a hidden acre, an ache
or a care, is it, what I hear, this seize,
the sea? Go forth, Worldling—.Come home—.
A mother knows and doesn't tell—

she demonstrates. This is how I leave the world—
I doe it while working at the loom, deer
ones, & through the cobwebs sweeps a broom—.
Fate is one way to spell faith wrong...
a winter bee in a spider's web how can it be
but so it bee. Warp and weft and a wastrel memory—
faith is one way to spell fate wrong...
myths fill a mother's mouth when the world is
weird woods, an endless form of what could
bee will be. Sick unto death but I didn't
die. I don't dye. I make soap from lye
and tell all the truth. There are witches, Worldlings,

with scissors and thread and a single I. The world
is weird, Darnings, a little tangle of eternal flame.
Winter dreams of ferns between birch and pine—
give it time, Hourlings, and the dream is true.
Like the dove I coo, sit on the brood &
brood. Even when there's work to do—
the pox that stains the cheek reminds the mind
how mercy carries a rod. I like to think God
doesn't think, but does the work God's meant to doe.
So soft the thistle after the purple after the pain.
A broom sweeps wisdom away. *Again* is the word
the inward mouth prays. Husband, children, *again*

the blood goes into the hearth and out
the blood goes again. Smoke of the ark
when the wood is green, crow's caa &
dove's woe & owl's who
are you now. You & the cloud of Exodus
fills the living room & the babies cough
their omens sharp as arrows in a vein.
Even the veilings sing. Venus in the evening.
The full moan. Lucifer waiting for the yawn
to unfold dark wings. Such youth
I've known groan old as Methuselah &
Lazarus takes a nap, a dog whining & licking

his bare toe. Blood woos and blood woes—
a kind apostasy from long ago pulses in the wife-
I-am's wrist. A kind of smoke within the
wood before the flame is woke. & the dear
flee before they know. They doe
their deaths in ways I pale cheek have no face
but in the earth I walk they go. A tear
should tear in half the cheek but no—. It don't—.
Spell woe wrong and wring it into love...
& then peace turns every verb into a doe asleep
in the woulds of her mother's ear.
Hush the owl hush the dove hush hush the crow

awe is the grammar of the awefull wilds
where I made a house that God burnt down.
It's odd, Oddments, faith—. So old &
yet it's never taken a breath—. That's why
belief don't cry—. It don't know how to yet—.
Nor exactly doe Eye. Have you ever
seen it as I have? The doe on the edge of
the woods, the dark holes of her eyes & nose,
& the ears' sudden lightning tuned to
who? It must be you but who is you? A burr
in the January cold. Spent some of our hours
in eternity darning in a sock a hole.

The Amory of the Syllable: A Brief Epilogue

"Blessed Bee, Dearest Deer" takes courage from John Berryman's *An Homage to Mistress Bradstreet.* That book's dense, consistent form, its thicket of music, eccentrically tracing Anne Bradstreet's ancestry, progeny, and biography, continues to pulse with contemporary poetic life—as does Anne Bradstreet's poetry itself. Among her poems, "As loving Hind," is my favorite. Nearly metaphysical in its metaphoric complexity, touching glancingly upon the touchstones of the past (notably Sir Thomas Wyatt "Whose List to Hunt," though wondrously reversing the tenor of his conceit), in rhyming couplets of iambic pentameter, Bradstreet offers us an ongoing lesson of the ways in which a poem of remarkable propriety can also be an engine of utmost desire. Here, the poem might mimic the life it masks: a seventeenth century woman, wife, and mother's life entwined within the wilds of New World. The loose variations of spelling and capitalization any student of early American Literature recognizes as marker of the literary epoch, gain in Anne Bradstreet's poems something that includes, but exceeds, the age's lexical idiosyncrasy. The poems, read honestly, might come to any given reader's ears as a marvel of excess that borders on the erotic. I like to think that the polysemic complexity inherent in Bradstreet's practice isn't simply a naïve relic of the time, but a wise and purposeful play that codes our inmost human complexity within a poetry that knows how "to behave." The mother that desires. The faithful one who doubts. The one within who only wants out. The believer who feels the affront of what she believes. A kind God who is so cruel; a cruel God who is so kind . . . How reconcile the opposites? Bradstreet gives us a wondrous answer: you don't. You simply learn to write poems that obey the Law and dismantle it at the same time. As if such a thing were simple. Maybe it is; maybe it's not. But what is true, to me now undeniably so, is that a poem can hold within itself many poems; a word can enfold within itself many words; and a syllable, so small a sound, is a wilderness entire. I love to think that Anne Bradstreet is at the very root of the poetry I'm learning even now to practice—a wild domesticity, a humility which loves the desire that riddles it, saying no to nothing, or turning *no* to *know*, where the apophatic becomes the episteme, that learns to say, as life always says, *yes* and *no* simultaneously forever. Not an either/or, but a both, but an also, but an *& & &*—

Kimberly L. Becker

Negative Space in Anne Bradstreet

What interests me most in the work of Anne Bradstreet is the negative space, what she does not discuss. As a writer, I know much of my writing is remarkable for what it doesn't say, what doesn't come into play, either because of my failure to observe or because of my lack of courage in naming the unspoken. But the unspoken in Bradstreet speaks loudly to me these many years later. For despite the variety of her poems and topics, she never addresses the colonial politics of Indigenous peoples. She ignores the Indians in her midst.

As a mixed-heritage poet, including and identifying Cherokee, although not an enrolled member of a sovereign nation, I want to write into that negative space, speaking the silence, putting words to the blankness of the page surrounding Bradstreet's ink. I invite attention to the negative space. Perhaps it isn't fair to judge someone retroactively (cancel culture may come for us all). But in contrast to Bradstreet's reticence, even willful ignorance, I think of Anna Akhmatova's willing witness: "Can you describe this? I can."

Why does anyone write? I remember Tillie Olsen: *every woman who writes is a survivor.* Bradstreet was, in her own way, a survivor, but not in the way we talk about survivors today, whether of abuse, boarding schools, intergenerational or historical trauma. But should she be judged retroactively? Should her work be disparaged for its domesticity, its solipsism? How easy for me to type these damning-with-faint-praise lines on my laptop. How difficult was it for her to summon her voice to write?

Anne Bradstreet wrote to document her own private life and loss, but obviously sought—and won—a wider audience, despite feigning ignorance of self-promotion. Even the great contemporary feminist poet Adrienne Rich has affirmed Anne Bradstreet as the first female poet of the New World. And yet words used to contextualize her work go unexamined: *Wilderness, New World.* The world may have been wild and new to the colonists. It was neither wild nor new to the original inhabitants.

Anne Bradstreet Now. Abram Van Engen and Mary Eyring, Oxford University Press.
 DOI: 10.1093/9780197811191.003.0005

Bradstreet is most certainly not "the first poet in the New World." Indian song and ceremony came first. I once visited Rome with a person who declared that civilization started with the Western world, when things were written down—a prejudiced and privileged view. Yet in Cherokee tradition, the most sacred things are *never* written down. They are passed on orally only to those who have earned the right to hear and eventually pass along to someone worthy of that legacy. Tension rises between knowing and writing, hearing and learning. Sometimes negative space is sacred space.

It can be difficult to read Bradstreet's work in the context of all the evils Europeans brought to the so-called Wilderness and the so-called New World. It is especially difficult when those evils continue in the form of racism and cultural genocide today. We need to remember, now and always: there were already civilizations of Native Americans living here, and their world was invaded.

In my professional life I have trained in trauma-informed care. The idea is not to judge and thereby retraumatize those who come seeking help. No doubt Bradstreet's life in "New" England in the "New" world was hard. Privilege may have insulated her: she was educated, she had means, she had the luxury to write. Even so, she was always aware of her lower status as a woman. In contrast, when Cherokee leader Attakullakulla met with an English negotiating party in 1765, various clan mothers and matriarchs were with him. The English men came alone. Attakullakulla asked them, "Where are your women?"

Certainly Bradstreet endured hardship. Her most vivid poem is about her house burning down, and she suffered ills and ailments all her life. But nothing she experienced was like the hardship endured by Native Americans upon the arrival of the colonists or the forced arrival of slaves. Again, what is interesting about Bradstreet is what she *didn't* write about. The white of the page. The negative space. The caesura in between cognitions. The lacunae of observation of what was actually happening historically. If we live forward, but understand only backward, maybe our (my) judgment of her literary merit softens. Maybe it sharpens.

I read Bradstreet backward, knowing the history to which she was not privy. Or was it that her privilege prevented her, as it does many today, from seeing what was right before her eyes? Perhaps her life of illness and motherhood circumscribed her private world so much that she could not afford to consider other people's lives. She had some kind of sympathy for the Roman Catholic Church, yet none for the Indians on whom Christianity was forced.

Who gets to tell the story? Who controls narratives? Always the dominant culture, while the sung songs, stories told in firelight, hum in the background, only understood by those who take time to learn and listen and upon whom another, secret, privilege is bestowed.

Of course, Indians have always had spirituality and ways of prayers. My Cherokee teacher always used to tell our class that when white people saw Natives around a fire, they saw savages worshiping fire. Instead, Indians were worshipping the fire gifted by the Creator and the fire in their hearts placed there by the Creator. The Cherokee practice of going to water predates Christian baptism. Even the translation of the Bible into Algonquin language seems unknown to Bradstreet. Or was it merely unremarked? Should we judge a poet for what is left out of her, his, or their opus? Was it simple oversight or intentional slight? What of writers today? What of myself?

This anthology about Anne Bradstreet indicates that she has held, does hold, an important place in American literature. She is known because she took pen to paper in a particular time, when it was unusual for a woman to do so. Bradstreet was surviving the best she could under difficult circumstances, lifting up her voice. But nothing she faced was as difficult as the original peoples of the "new" world or "new" England. The English wanted a different iteration, but they carried with them (as did some of my ancestors) the hubris of thinking they had solved everything with their religion.

Can we ever trust any poet that writes from a place of absolute conviction in any dogma or doctrine? What is left when we pare away our inherited religion, our unexamined prejudices, our fear of being unheard, unknown? What negative space resides within each of us that propels us to carve out a work of art that is ours alone to offer? In the book *Art and Fear*, David Bayles and Ted Orland caution: "fears about yourself prevent you from doing your best work, while fears about your reception by others prevent you from doing your own work."

What fears did Bradstreet encounter? What fears does any poet or artist encounter? Fear is relegated to that negative space until it demands attention. Bradstreet's fears were domestic, circumscribed. As I write, I fear for our next election, for the effects of climate change, for the lack of housing or healthcare for so many, for women's reproductive rights. Some of my fears push their way into my work, but some I hold back, because to write about fears might feed them instead of taming them. In *The Places That Scare You*, Pema Chödrön writes:

May we continue to open our hearts and minds, in order to work ceaselessly for the benefit of all beings.
May we go to the places that scare us.
May we lead the life of a warrior.

Perhaps the best strength of Bradstreet's work is to invite us to examine the way language is used, what it names and what it ignores, and what the naming and ignoring might do—how it acts. Perhaps her poetry can be a caution not to ignore or discount the negative spaces of our lives.

In my professional capacity, I wrote a grant for environmental reparations for a North Dakota tribal community whose ancestral land was flooded by a government-built dam that occasioned yet again the breaking of a US treaty. In the Southeast, Cherokee land was flooded by TVA. This is recent history. Can I describe this? Yes, I can.

Poets are citizens of a wider country than oneself, than one's nation. If our words are too personal they don't touch the bottom of the lake; if too general, they merely skate across the surface. Do I demand too much of Bradstreet? Do I, from my own place of privilege, have the right to look askance from this great distance of time and history?

I am a common reader of Bradstreet's work. I think of her aboard the *Arbella* as she observed waves and gulls and dolphins and the occasional shark or even whale. The gray expanse of ocean occasioned perhaps her first welling up of emotion that she would then commit to poetry. Hers was a chosen journey, a cosseted journey. Arduous in its way, but not enforced.

Bradstreet's poetry can become an interesting exercise to interrogate our assumptions and privileges. Her poetry might inadvertently embolden us to look unflinchingly. At ourselves. At our world. Then to compose our own art, with a thoughtful, if painful, balance of negative and positive space.

Sophie Cabot Black

What I meant to say was

(Anne Bradstreet, Andover Massachusetts, Autumn 1669)

Let the house burn again;
Already I outlive the New World,
The last dog dead, one cow
Remnant in the gleaning wind

Of leaf-fall and each child left
For elsewhere. To stay
Past those I buried; I do not know
What more to spend—

The government of man
By man brings no one home.
No longer do I want
To be upon this hill,

This place of so much wind
Where I keep writing
Past the end. I have broken
Each sentence, halved

Then half again, each word
Simpled down like old oxen
Kept as if to cover
The whole field, turn

Anne Bradstreet Now. Abram Van Engen and Mary Eyring, Oxford University Press.
 DOI: 10.1093/9780197811191.003.0006

By turn. Now the words
Come less, the clouds so fast
And not what I thought
I thought. For what

Have I survived:
To save each house,
A door sprung open, plain,
Willing each hinge

To work, verse
By verse to outlast,
Outlove whatever it is
You bring forth.

This poem, in the voice of Anne Bradstreet toward the end of her life, shows signs of a struggle with how to reconcile what she has been taught with what she intuits. Bradstreet's life has alternately been filled with faith and doubt, with light and shadow, in a tension between the known and the unknowable.

In this piece, I wanted to capture the New England the poet would have lived in over her decades, with its stages of change, of renewal and demise. I saw her daily stitching a life for her family out of the relentless wilderness, while on her tongue the words from her bible chimed. And as she paid attention on how to be of use, as "visible saint," as mother, wife, and poet, Bradstreet found herself a still point as the patterns of a vaster world swirled round her, each season bringing its changes of weather, of habit, and of hope.

In an early draft, the last line of "What I Meant to Say" landed on the more immediate and visceral:

> "the leaves fully gone
> and each tree in a cold tremble."

But for me this ending had not captured the tension I thought important, of the intentional removal Bradstreet's family had made to beat some edge in service to their beliefs. And so the last line became more explicit, aimed at the "You" she prayed to, wondered at, gathered in the name of. My own New England family had grown up without God, without organized religion; we saw ourselves as living inside nature, not out. And with Anne Bradstreet, having lived so close to the unknown while also cleaving to such strict scripture, I wanted to weave in her turnings, both away, and toward.

And so the last lines then became:

> "I admit nothing
> save to be noticed;
> to what end: just to see
> if he would show?"

While this line somewhat captured what I was aiming at, the "he" was too small, too distanced, and so "he" becomes a "you." And too I realized I wanted her last line here to convey an overcoming of doubt—and for a while (as I worked through the rest of the poem over months and months) it read:

> "living, loving you all the way through."

And then a later version:

> "willing to outlove,
> outlast you all the way through."

Yet still these lines did not hold the idea of the inbetween, the thin place where the human lives in both conviction and wonder, in that dialectic. And so came the final:

> "To work, verse
> By verse to outlast,
> Outlove whatever it is
> You bring forth."

When I shared this with a dear friend, who grew up Catholic and still has a strong belief system, she insisted I replace the word "you" with the word "God." I struggled with the idea: again as I had not been brought up with such a tradition, or reverence for the use of that particular word (the word "God"), I thought this was too restrictive, and felt using "God" would limit the reader. I wanted the word to be both a "You" and a "you." I wanted the reader to feel the overtones of the "Self" up against whatever "Other" is encountered; to feel Bradstreet, especially toward the end of her life, wrestling with self-reliance and self-doubt, with the pragmatic and the precarious. Imagining Bradstreet and what she considered, in this vast "new world" fraught with unencountered flora and fauna—one filled with her husband's departures, the birth and death of children, the gathering of harvests—there needed to be tension in the penultimate line. The line asks the reader to both hear her self-determination, yet also to read (in undertone) the idea that she is *telling* the reader to join her in this directive, even challenge, to "Outlove whatever it is."

Another aspect of the final ending shows how poetry can be used to work out multiple meanings using line breaks, using the white space of a page. Poetry differs from prose in many ways, one of which is how the poet can posit words, meter, syntax, line breaks, in such ways a reader is forced to think differently than in prose; in this poem, the final line breaks in such a way that the "you" gets to be capitalized, which gives the "you," now a "You," a more profound presence.

This poem speaks to the paring down at the end of a life, of writing poetry, of physical labor, of keeping a family alive, of understanding whatever is "ungodly," while at the same time to hold, and represent, even love, the contradictions, the messiness of the world.

Sophie Cabot Black
October 2024

Daniel Borzutzky

{Dis} Temper

In anguish of my heart replete with woes,
And wasting pains which best my body knows...
Anne Bradstreet, "Upon Some Distemper of Body"

1

Here is a hollow organ

Here is a hollow muscular organ that by its rhythmic contraction acts as a force pump maintaining the circulation of blood

Here is a hollow muscular organ that pumps blood and is enclosed or surrounded by something ELSE

To be enclosed or surrounded by something else, to indicate the quality of something, to incorporate, to be in an appropriate place, to be located inside of, or within, to be in a position, in an operation, in power

The boss is in the fix is in high-waisted jeans are in I was in control of the situation until my hollow muscular organ exploded

Here is a hollow muscular organ that serves as the emotional center of a body, it is also where courage or anguish is located...

Anguish, from the Old French:

anguisse, angoisse.

Anne Bradstreet Now. Abram Van Engen and Mary Eyring, Oxford University Press.
 DOI: 10.1093/9780197811191.003.0007

A "choking sensation, distress, anxiety, rain"

angustia:

Did the muscular organ feel tightness, straitness, narrowness? Was it troubled or distressed?

To get inside the hollow muscular organ and to attempt to know what another person is feeling

They say you can only understand your own body after you have understood the body of another

What did they mean?

Nevertheless, we must penetrate this muscular organ

It is filled with something, it is uncontainable

There is not a standard English word for these sensations

If you can provide more information or context...

We may be able to help you understand what you are feeling

Yes, if you can provide the muscular organ with more information or context...

To be abundantly fed, to be full or filled or abundantly provided for

The muscular organ is filled with something shared between many languages

Unfortunately, you and I don't speak any of them

When a body is filled with grief, regret, or distress—sounds come out of it—sounds that the body cannot always control

(Everyone knows that babies cry in different languages)

Here is my hollow organ

Here is my muscular organ

I washed my face and all I saw were blemishes

I washed my face and all I saw was dread

2

Here is a hollow organ in the trunk of a beast

Here is a hollow organ in the physical structure of a human or animal

Here is a material frame, the material existence of the human, the main or principal part of anything

Was the phrase "over my dead body" first written by Coleridge in his translation of a play by Schiller?

Body politic or body image or body count or body language or body snatcher

"No Monster! First over my dead body thou shalt treat"

To be enclosed or surrounded by something else, to indicate the quality of something, to incorporate, to be in an appropriate place, to be located inside of, or within, to be in a position, in an operation, in power

Thereupon (I lay waste), next (I lay waste), and so forth (I lay waste) and so on

(Which..........which............which)

Wasting

From the Latin *vastus:* empty, desolate

To lose strength or health, to pine, to weaken

Gastar, guastare

Devastating, undergoing or causing decay or losing strength

Still, we must penetrate the muscular organ

To be abundantly fed, to be full or filled or abundantly provided for

Deuteronomy 28:22: The LORD will strike you with wasting disease and with fever, inflammation and fiery heat, and with drought and with blight and with mildew. They shall pursue you until you perish

Leviticus 26:16: I will bring terror on you—wasting disease and fever that will cause your eyes to fail and your life to ebb away. You will sow your seed in vain because your enemies will eat it

Job 16:8: It has come up as a witness against me, and the wasting of my flesh makes answer to my face

The question is simple:

Why are you so sad? And why when you are sad does your body feel as if it is decaying, or losing strength?

The hollow organ is filled with something that is shared between many breathers

Excuse me, is that a grenade in your muscular organ?

A small bomb?

Subdue the earth, already, would you

I had a thought while penetrating your muscular organ:

When was the very first massacre?

When was the second massacre?

I get distracted when I think of the relationship between the author and her book

"A choking sensation, distress, anxiety, rain"

Does the one thing feed the other?

Or is the thing that holds us together only a means of extracting further information from a source or connecting one material body to another

A body of knowledge

Or a knowledge of a body in pain

Pain, a word first articulated in the fourteenth century

Connected to the word punishment

The opposite of pleasure

Mental or emotional suffering, grief, distress

Hell's torments

Here, kid:

Take this money as compensation for all the blood that has been spilled in the previous centuries

Retraction or penalty or retribution

He enjoyed the ways in which physical discomfort allowed for him to be able to access his most intimate thoughts and feelings

Or

She had a healthy means of coping with her distress that in other bodies might have led to extreme depression or debilitation

An overwhelming bodily sensation induced by a noxious stimulus

To accept it, to integrate it into one's daily life

Let us talk about a pulsing pressure upon naked nerve endings

Let us talk about the relationship between the state's bombs, the bank's money, and the subject's body?

What do you mean when you say: your body knows best?

What she means is that she holds the ability to distinguish between familiar sensations and unfamiliar ones, between shattering sensations and unshattering ones, between the entire physical structure of the human animal and the little bits of this and that which make life a little bit more or less worth living

Who said that and what did they mean?

This is my hollow muscular organ

I can distinguish it from your hollow muscular organ

But if I am honest I can scarcely distinguish what I feel from what I know

Knowledge, gnosis, cognition, ignorance

I can scarcely distinguish what I am from what I owe

INCOGNITO

Unknown, not investigated

A strange word in the silence of a beast

A breath, an inquiry, a moan or murmur

It's just that I can't sleep when my heart hurts

And when my heart hurts I feel a disturbance, a distemper

An unnatural temper, a balance upset or disturbed

A malady of the body

The wasting disease of a young dog

This song should be called:

Fill this hole with the wasting flash of your body

Eduardo C. Corral

Arbella

The bedding reeks
   of windfall apples—
when I sleep, I'm back
   in an orchard. My neck
needled by insects,
   black fruit caving
in the sun, &
   swaying branches . . .

It's the swaying
   that wakes me.
The ship endlessly
   pitching, the three masts
rocking in unison
   like the devout. Yesterday,
I saw a seasick woman
   gazing

at the larger mast
   as she uttered
a prayer. A provocation,
   a breach. I must not envy her
need to bring in
   the manmade
into her conversation with God.
   What I profess is

knowable by uncallable.
   Under my tongue,

Anne Bradstreet Now. Abram Van Engen and Mary Eyring, Oxford University Press.
 DOI: 10.1093/9780197811191.003.0008

repugnant salt
pork bits, tint
of astringest smoke. On deck,
sprays of seawater
cool my face, slow
the wheels

of hungry. Others
spend hours by the handrail,
eyes drifting in search
of the Talbot,
the Ambrose. Even windstorms
cannot evict
the seabirds nesting
in barrels, in buckets. I never

linger too long on deck.
I scurry, I rustle—
what sustains rots. Rigging,
planks, faith.

Joanne Diaz

"Too Many My Diseases to Recite": Anne Bradstreet's Illness Narratives[1]

I was born and raised in a place where I ought to have known a great deal about Anne Bradstreet. I grew up in Billerica, Massachusetts, and throughout my young life, I could feel the thrum of literary history in the towns all around me. In middle school, our teachers took us to Cambridge on a field trip to the house of Henry Wadsworth Longfellow. In high school, right after I got my driver's license, I drove to Author's Ridge at the Sleepy Hollow Cemetery in Concord, where my friends and I visited the graves of Ralph Waldo Emerson and Henry David Thoreau. Multiple times in college, I went to Lowell for the annual Jack Kerouac Festival, and once, I watched Allen Ginsberg sing William Blake's "Nurse's Song" as he played his tiny concertina in an auditorium at UMass Lowell.

In a state like Massachusetts, every other street bears a historical marker for a person or event that transformed the history of that place, so how could I have missed America's first published poet? It wasn't as if my path had not crossed hers. For years, we'd drive to Andover to visit my brother, who graduated from Merrimack College, just down the street from where Bradstreet's home originally stood. My family regularly brought out-of-towners to Woodman's of Essex, where we'd devour plates of fried fish. After lunch, we'd go to Crane Beach, where I'd collect shells and watch clams bubble up from the sand flats, all just a few miles down the street from Ipswich, where Anne Bradstreet lived for a time. As an adult, whenever I hurried past the Harvard Gate, browsed for books at the Grolier Book Shop, or watched people play checkers outside of the Au Bon Pain in Harvard Square, I was standing just a few feet from where Anne Bradstreet first lived, in what was then called Newtown, and later, Cambridge. But never once in all of

[1] From Anne Bradstreet, "Of the Four Ages of Man," l. 225. *The Works of Anne Bradstreet*, ed. Jeannine Hensley (Belknap, 2010).

Anne Bradstreet Now. Abram Van Engen and Mary Eyring, Oxford University Press.
 DOI: 10.1093/9780197811191.003.0009

those years did a teacher mention her name: not when I was a child, not in college, and not even in graduate school many years later.

When I finally did engage with Bradstreet's work, my readings were poor and presumptuous. I saw her as a pious Puritan writing occasional poems: upon the burning of her house, upon the births and deaths of her family members, upon the publication of her famous collection *The Tenth Muse*. By her own admission, she was a didactic poet: her goal was to instruct and provide a model of Puritan devotion that might guide her children for years to come.[2] What she said about her own work confirmed what I thought I knew, and commentary by contemporary authors only reinforced my assumptions. Even Adrienne Rich, whose treatment of Bradstreet's work is so poignant and insightful, dismisses her poetry as "curiously impersonal" and rather conventional in its articulations.[3]

But now, as I slow down and attend to her work more carefully, I see my error. What I did not know was that Bradstreet was in and out of illness and various kinds of distress for her entire adult life: smallpox, the threats of malnutrition and starvation, infertility, various states of pregnancy for almost twenty years, grief over the loss of various family members, chronic pain, fainting, and fatigue, and ultimately tuberculosis—a "consumption" that "wasted her to skin and bone" and led to her death.[4] Much of her life in America was one of dis-ease; indeed, her quote that is inscribed on the Bradstreet Gate at Harvard University reads: "I came into this country where I found a new world and new manners at which my heart rose." Though "my heart rose" sounds like a description of her enthusiasm, she uses that phrase to indicate her shocked and perhaps even nauseated response to her life in this new place.[5]

What does it mean for America's first poet to be a woman so concerned with chronic bodily suffering? In her poems about illness, she seems utterly devoted to a God who might provide her with some consolation, and perhaps even amelioration, of her suffering. But one can also see the "stress marks

[2] Bradstreet wrote to her children, "I have not studied in this you read to show my skill, but to declare the Truth, not to set forth my self, but the glory of God." Jeanine Hensley, "Anne Bradstreet's Wreath of Thyme" in *The Works of Anne Bradstreet*, xxxiv.

[3] Adrienne Rich, "Anne Bradstreet and Her Poetry." *The Works of Anne Bradstreet*, xxi. Rich herself lived with a number of painful chronic conditions, including rheumatoid arthritis, and refers to her own "chronic lameness" when reflecting upon Bradstreet's work, even as she is dismissive of its value. Cynthia R. Wallace's wonderful essay sheds some light on how Rich's illness and disability inform her poetry and criticism: "'The Problem Is / to Connect': Adrienne Rich, Chronic Disease, and the Risky Solidarities of Pain." *New England Review* 45.2 (2024): 61–76.

[4] Hensley, li.

[5] Molly Farrell, "Disgusting Affects from the Antinomian Controversy to the Antiabortion Movement." *American Literature* 90.4 (2018): 785–813, 808.

of anger" and "the strains of self-division" that indicate a poetic speaker in real distress.[6] And while these poems of illness might be didactic, they are also pointing to the inadequacy of the devotional lyric modes of her time. Bradstreet's poems about illness attempt to spiritualize her physical ailments and transform them into something meaningful; even so, she reveals a frustration that is ancient and foundational to all lamentation texts. While there is no doubt that Bradstreet is a pious Puritan, she is also deeply frustrated with the hold that illness has on her, and she regularly interrogates God's motives in her work. Bradstreet's use of rhetorical questions, commands, exclamations, and repetitions foregrounds her embittered stance and creates a poetics of correction and confinement. In doing so, Bradstreet points to the fragility of her relationship with God, even as she wants to solidify it.

Even when Bradstreet is not writing about illness in a literal way, she is describing her poetry with metaphors of illness. In "The Author to Her Book," she deploys a familiar posture of modesty and describes her poetry in terms of its physical deficiencies. In her view, the poems are the "ill-formed offspring of [her] feeble brain": monstrous, undisciplined, ugly, and full of "defects" (1, 14). Throughout the poem, she continues to anticipate her reader's objections to her poetic lines by figuring them as disabled. When describing her prosody, for example, she writes, "I stretched thy joints to make thee even feet, / Yet still thou run'st more hobbling than is meet" (16–17).

Just as she points to the "illness" of her prosody, so too does she point to the illness of her body and spirit, to a God that ought to give meaning to that suffering, and then to his silence as an absence of meaning. This notion of pointing to one's own body in illness was common enough among early modern poets and painters: in the early 1500s, when Albrecht Dürer fell ill, he drew this iconic illustration of himself and sent it to his physician in order to better describe his pain (see Figure 1):

At the top of the illustration, Dürer wrote: "Do wo der gelb fleck is und mit dem finger drawff dewt do is mir we" (There, where the yellow spot is located, and where I point my finger, there it hurts").[7] This desire to point, and to thus create a clear map of illness, was not uncommon figuration among male poets: in "Hymn to My God, My God in My Sickness," John

[6] "Anne Bradstreet and Her Poetry," xxi.

[7] To learn more about this drawing, see G. D. Schott, "*The Sick Dürer*—A Renaissance Prototype Pain Map." *BMJ* (2004): 329. https://www.bmj.com/content/329/7480/1492.1 Accessed 6 September 2024.

Figure 1 Albrecht Dürer, *Self-Portrait,* 1521.
Kunsthalle, Bremen.

Donne compares his sick body to a "flat map" and guides the physician toward the pain.[8] Elsewhere, Ben Jonson and George Herbert lament the limitations and ultimate decline of the human body. But how could a woman poet in Puritan New England possibly point to her body in that way? Throughout the sixteenth and seventeenth centuries, theologians regularly aligned illness of the body with illness of the soul, and women's bodies were perceived as leaky, incomplete vessels that were an embarrassment to be contained and managed.[9] No woman poet in literary history would have felt more keenly the despair associated with sin, and the profound burden that any Puritan subject might have felt when both sick at heart *and* sick in body. As biographer Charlotte Gordon notes, Bradstreet had smallpox at the age of sixteen, and when she did, "she perceived her suffering as punishment for her passion. Later in life, she wrote, 'It hath been with me that no sooner felt my heart out of order, but I have expected correction for it,' and in this case she connected the fact that she had allowed 'the follies of youth [to] take hold of me' with her illness."[10]

[8] *The Norton Anthology of English Literature,* 7th ed., Volume 1, ed. M. H. Abrams and Stephen Greenblatt (Norton, 2000).

[9] Gail Kern Paster, *The Body Embarrassed: Drama and the Disciplines of Shame in Early Modern England* (Cornell University Press, 1993).

[10] Bradstreet qtd. in Charlotte Gordon, *Mistress Bradstreet: The Untold Life of America's First Poet* (Little, Brown and Company, 2005), 48–49.

To solve this problem of embarrassment and piety, Bradstreet relied upon the lamentation tradition that she would have known from the Psalms. Lamentation was considered one of the highest forms of poetic expression, providing a kind of catharsis for readers and writers. As George Puttenham notes:

> Lamenting is altogether contrary to rejoising, every man saith so, and yet is it a peece of joy to be able to lament with ease, and freely to poure forth a mans inward sorrowes and the greefs wherewith his minde is surcharged. This was a very necessary devise of the Poet and a fine, besides his poetrie to play also the Phisitian, and not onely by applying a medicine to the ordinary sicknes of mankind, but by making the very greef it selfe (in part) cure of the disease.[11]

In Puttenham's theory of poetry, the excesses of poetic lamentation can provide a salve for the despairing reader or writer. Puttenham endorses the use of excessive emotion in poetry as a remedy for excessive emotion in life, a suggested remedy that appears in numerous treatments for grief and melancholy in the period.

Embedded in every lamentation is an invective in which the mourning subject rails against forces beyond his or her control, and this is why it's such a valuable mode of expression for Bradstreet. Consider "For Deliverance from a Fever." In this poem, the poetic speaker is suffering with physical ailments that confine and constrain her, and she hopes that by appealing to God, she might find some relief. The poem begins with a description of the symptoms that envelop her body and spirit:

> When sorrows had begirt me round
> And pains within and out,
> When in my flesh no part was found
> Then didst Thou rid me out.
> My burning flesh in sweat did boil,
> My aching head did break,
> From side to side for ease I toil,
> So faint I could not speak. (1–8)

[11] *The arte of English poesie Contriued into three bookes: the first of poets and poesie, the second of proportion, the third of ornament* (London: Richard Field, 1589), 37.

Bradstreet's use of the fourteener—the four-beat line followed by a three-beat line across multiple lines and stanzas—might initially give this poem a sing-songy feel, but notice the sense of profound confinement that it exacerbates in the poem. The fourteener was the channel through which lamentation psalms were set to melodies in the Bay Psalm Psalter; it was also the centuries-old ballad meter used to tell stories of ordinary people in extraordinary circumstances. "Begirt" suggests surrounding or encircling. If one were "begirt," one would hope it would be with a belt that has a weapon attached to it.[12] In these poetic lines, though, sorrow is the weapon that "pains [her] within and without." There is no part of the speaker that is not suffused with a pain that leaves her utterly bereft.

The next quatrains take a distinctly juridical turn in which the poetic speaker is like the accused in a court of law who is trying to understand why she is being punished:

> Beclouded was my soul with fear
> Of Thy displeasure sore,
> Nor could I read my evidence
> Which oft I read before.
> "Hide not Thy face from me!" I cried,
> From burnings keep my soul.
> Thou know'st my heart, and hast me tried;
> I on Thy mercies roll." (10–17)

Because the speaker's soul is "beclouded," she is unable to clearly see the "evidence" that would indict her. She knows that the illness must be a sign of God's displeasure, but with what? Bradstreet is Job-like in her lamentation, searching for some fault in herself—fault that she has found multiple times in the past—and finding none. If there is no way to know <u>why</u> she's suffering, if there's no meaning that she can make from her illness, then is she in a godless place with no redemption? Her frustration with this possibility is so palpable that she urgently exclaims: "Hide not Thy face from me!" (14). The speaker's exclamation demands clarity and vividness of evidence, but God provides none. She knows that God has offered mercy in the past, and yet the consistency of that mercy is put into question by its "rolling" quality. "Rolling"

[12] "begirt," v. *Oxford English Dictionary*, Oxford University Press, July 2023, https://doi.org/10.1093/OED/3427924072. *The Oxford English Dictionary*. Accessed 6 September 2024.

might initially suggest a gentle motion, but in this context, it describes a "rocking, often violently, from side to side," as if the speaker is on a turbulent boat ride, rather than the consistency of God's love.[13] The poem points to—and provides a critique of—the instability of God's mercy.

When God finally does hear Bradstreet's prayer, he removes his rod and spares her frail body, suggesting a severe, Old Testament God who uses corporal punishment upon his people. Now that God is showing Bradstreet some tenderness through recovery, her heart will no longer "quail," or waste away. The alignment of "frail" and "quail" is suggestive—here is an instance of where Bradstreet's body, though "frail," might not "quail," bird-like, but grow and even thrive again. The final stanza of the poem seems to conclude on a positive note of praise and adulation:

> O, praises to my mighty God,
> Praise to my Lord, I say,
> Who hath redeemed my soul from pit,
> Praises to Him for aye. (26–29)

The "For aye," or "forever," at the end of the stanza initially registers as eternal gratitude and praise, but this is one of those instances where reading a poem in its context can be instructive. Consider "From Another Sore Fit," the poem that immediately follows "Deliverance from a Fever." In this poem, Bradstreet once again refers to God's "rod" of punishment (15); and in the next poem, "Deliverance from a Fit of Fainting," notice how the poem begins in a posture of defeat and exhaustion:

> Worthy art Thou, O Lord, of praise,
> But ah! It's not in me.
> My sinking heart I pray Thee raise
> So shall I give it Thee.
>
> My life as spider's webb's cut off
> Thus fainting have I said,
> And living man no more shall see
> But be in silence laid. [1–8]

[13] "roll, *V.* (2), Sense I.1.a." *Oxford English Dictionary*, Oxford University Press, March 2024, https://doi.org/10.1093/OED/1603088181. Accessed 6 September 2024.

In these lines, the poetic speaker acknowledges that God is worthy of praise, but she is so fatigued by recurrent illness that she cannot offer it: "But ah! It's not in me." This acknowledgment of defeat, followed by a request for help, followed by eventual recovery, is a pattern that Bradstreet deploys numerous times; each time, though, there's the unsettling sense that her prayers will end in frustration. In the final stanza of this poem, Bradstreet writes, "Why should I live but to thy praise? / My life is hid with thee" (13–14). This *percontatio,* or rhetorical question, is commonly employed "for purposes of rhetorical effect instead of a positive statement,"[14] but why does she ask it? Bradstreet uses the *percontatio* in her journal entries, too: on July 8, 1656, after describing a "sore fit of fainting, which lasted 2 or 3 days," she writes, "O Lord, let me never forget Thy goodness, nor question Thy faithfulness to me, for Thou art my God, Thou hast said, and shall not I believe it?" (274). Elsewhere, in an entry dated May 11, 1657, Bradstreet describes a "sore sickness and weakness" that lasted for an entire season and prevented her from fully engaging in family life. She writes: "Who am I that I should repine at His pleasure, especially seeing it is for my spiritual advantage, for I hope my soul shall flourish while my body decays, and the weakness of this outward man shall be a means to strengthen my inner man" (278). Who am I to complain . . . and yet, here I am, complaining.

As Adrienne Rich observes, for the seventeenth century Puritan reader, "the final value of a poem lay in its revelation of God and not the individual,"[15] but if that's true, then the version of God revealed in these poems is punitive, juridical, and inconsistent in his mercy. Bradstreet's illness narratives are situated at the crossroads between devotion and frustration. At every turn, she aims to create pious poems that will serve as models for her children; every time, though, she faces the insufficiency of not only God's mercy but also her own attempts to express her frustration and despair.

My writing of this essay coincided with a trip back home to Massachusetts. As I returned to those sand flats, walked through Ipswich to find the historical marker for Bradstreet's house, and waded through tall grass to imagine where her Andover house once stood, I saw that the geography of that place is suffused with Bradstreet's lived experience. Before, I could only see a pious poet who spoke to the concerns of her time; now, I saw her poetry

[14] M. B. Parkes, *Pause and Effect: An Introduction to the History of Punctuation in the West* (University of California Press, 1993), 219.
[15] Rich, "Anne Bradstreet and Her Poetry," xiv.

as a kind of pain map directing me toward constellations of unresolved suffering. The pain was everywhere: in the briny ocean air, the tangles of seaweed, the sandy soil that must have made growing her garden full of medicinal herbs so difficult. As I saw this pain map evolve, I started to wonder how it might provide a model for other writers who have struggled to articulate the meaning of illness. How do Jane Kenyon's Eagle Pond, Audre Lorde's New York City, and Adrienne Rich's Santa Cruz provide constellations in which all points of illness inform and shape their writing? Perhaps, in this way, Bradstreet was speaking into the future, and her work can contribute to a now well-recognized corpus of illness narratives that shed light on "the kingdom of the sick."[16]

[16] Susan Sontag, *Illness as Metaphor* (Farrar, Straus and Giroux, 1977), 3.

Kathy Fagan

Anne Bradstreet and the Privately Radical Life of the Mind

In Ireland to visit my grandmother's home place and family, I met a local gentleman my age in a Dublin pub who, hearing I was born Irish Catholic American, locked eyes with me sympathetically and said: "You're living with a past you cannot know. It'll be on you all your life." We'd had a few pints. I asked if he were a psychotherapist; he was not.

My grandmother worked most of her life as a housecleaner and died before retiring from an assembly line job. She bought me, her only granddaughter, U.S. Savings Bonds when she could afford to, at least once a year. Her husband worked in the Coty factory until the inhalation of talc compromised his lungs. My paternal grandparents worked the railroad and "played the ponies." Both my blue-collar parents worked, moving around the country, restless, always in search of something. Something better, they said. I, too, wanted something I considered better; first-gen college, I worked my way through school and never left. On us all, all our lives.

I offer my own American narrative, so different from Bradstreet's, to point more honestly toward what we share: the condition of American women who write poems. To read John Berryman's *Homage to Mistress Bradstreet*, one might further distill that commonality to "American," the American nightmare of Berryman's and Rich's 1950s as disruptive to the soul as Bradstreet's immigration in the 1630s. Her heartsickness in the face of perilous threats surrounding her daily; Berryman's rage and Rich's activism in the face of McCarthyism, segregation, the Cold War, and gross proliferation of ongoing capitalist-colonialist priorities. Puritanical emphasis on faith, conformity, and individual exceptionalism fueled those priorities, but the inventions of cruelty and empire, monster twins born long before, thrived then and thrive now.

In the 1979 postscript to her foreword for Jeannine Hensley's Bradstreet edition, Adrienne Rich concludes: "I believe any woman for whom the

Anne Bradstreet Now. Abram Van Engen and Mary Eyring, Oxford University Press.
 DOI: 10.1093/9780197811191.003.0010

feminist breaking of silence has been a transforming force can also look back to a time when the faint, improbable outlines of unaskable questions, curling in her brain cells, triggered a shock of recognition at certain lines, phrases, images, in the work of this or that woman, long dead, whose life and experience she could only dimly try to imagine."

Arguably Rich and Bradstreet, both mothers (I am not), both from affluent, cultivated families, have more in common with each other than with me, but reading both again today indeed triggers in me shocks of recognition. That recognition lies first in the rhythms of our bodies, connected, of course, to the rhythms of domestic life—how one works on a poem, in the seventeenth century or the 20th or the 21st, while washing laundry, preparing a meal, tending to someone ill, or any number of other familial and community duties typically performed by women.

Rich is addressing something beyond the experiential, however: the "breaking of silence" that happens because of the act of poem-writing itself, the "transforming force" and "unaskable questions" products of keenly open and sensitive minds. The urge to read and write real poems requires a private radicalism in white American culture, radical enough to value engagement with both self and society without the promise of financial gain. In other words, radical enough to oppose capitalist agendas. That Rich and Berryman wrote political poems isn't news; that they recognized in Bradstreet the political may be. Her very doubts—about America, her faith, her body—constitute bold political rebellions modestly considered in her work, one likely reason the work lasts.

When I was a young poet, I knew of Bradstreet only through the Berryman poem. Rereading it now, I find so much more than his memorably idiosyncratic speech and unimpeachable craft. The poem presents new problems for me (male gaze and presumptions) it hadn't before, but also articulates a critique of America I couldn't fully hear over the interpersonal drama of the poem; I wasn't ready then to receive it. Given my background, I should have been ready. Berryman was my mentor's mentor—Philip Levine brilliantly valorized him in the essay "Mine Own John Berryman"—and Rich, a contemporary of Levine's, and one of the most awarded and maligned white women poets of her time, provoked in me, a baby queer, fear and awe. Nonetheless, I foolishly believed in my twenties and thirties that my life was then and would remain as far from theirs as from Bradstreet's. That history was linear. That my peers and I were confronting and creating something very new in post-post-Vietnam America. I was of course wrong. American foreign policy, racism, and sexism remain as disastrous and deadly as they ever were, and socioeconomic class structures shift but do not fundamentally change. The rich build their houses on the backs of the poor. On us all, all our lives.

In time I hope to think further about Conrad Aiken's inclusion of Bradstreet in his 1929 anthology. I hope to revisit the work of Edward Taylor. I wish to consider more thoroughly Bradstreet's peculiar interest in and tolerance for Catholicism. No doubt she found among the papists justifications for suffering like those of Puritanism, but what else there might she have found compelling? Given my constraints, however, I offer only this brief essay and a short domestic lyric in which I hope, were Bradstreet here today, she might find shocks of recognition: American landscape outside, an ordinary if unquiet mind inside, the constant concern for children, regard for home, and the specter of death. I think it a distant cousin to her short poems about love of family, loss of family, and grief for both her native homeland and the destruction of her house by fire in 1666. There's a puzzle in the poem the speaker can't remember she's solved; Bradstreet might recognize herself in that, too.

EQUIP

The arborist says the trees have met and accomplished a canopy
over my yard, as if it were their intention to provide shade,
or my own to train them, when all I'd intended was
to finish the hard wordle for which I had only E and I all day,
misplacing I four times before finding, well, U,
three vowels, one five letter word I've little need for,
so little I keep forgetting I'd solved it, finally, while chewing
an apple so crisp and sweet I didn't notice the rot until
I saw it, bee-brown after every bite: EQUIP:
word of the rich or of those intending to be,
trees laden with fruit the children cannot reach to eat.

Rigoberto González

Sor Juana's Sonnet to Anne Bradstreet: A Conceit

Firstly God, creator of all things earthly and divine,
sacred spark that breathes to life every thought or word
no matter how awkwardly phrased or risibly absurd,
let us praise the poetry of men, so imperfect yet sublime.

Let us also praise the ingenuity of woman's verse,
which without permission, though perhaps some obligation,
reassessed, reconfigured, and improved on the dictation
of those whose song and music staged went unrehearsed.

We are blessed, oh lady of the pious line, to be free
of the burden that plagues the mediocre learned male
who pines for recognition, praise, and ceremony.

Greatness comes to she who unassumingly travails
undisturbed in her asylum, library of intellect and livery
of long gown and a cap; or tunic, cincture, and a veil.

Anne Bradstreet Now. Abram Van Engen and Mary Eyring, Oxford University Press.
 DOI: 10.1093/9780197811191.003.0011

Linda Gregerson

Anne Bradstreet's Four Quartets

Like so many of her readers, John Berryman looks chiefly to the stimulant of Anne Bradstreet's biography, rather than to her poetry, for inspiration. In "Homage to Mistress Bradstreet," he presumes to speak in the poet's own voice about the project to which she devoted her earliest extended writing hours:

> Versing, I shroud among the dynasties;
> Quaternion on quaternion, tireless I phrase
> Anything past, dead, far,
> sacred, for a barbarous place.
>
> ("Homage," 12)

Bradstreet's *Quaternions,* four linked sequences of four parts each, are organized according to the divisions of creation, as understood by the ancient Greeks and elaborated by successive generations of natural philosophers: The Four Elements, The Four Humours in Man's Constitution, The Four Ages of Man, and The Four Seasons. Well might a highly educated Englishwoman, an ocean away from the cultured settings in which she had been raised, bound by faith and family to the hardships of a seventeenth century Puritan colony in Massachusetts, find structure for her thought and verse in so vested an inheritance. She might have found comfort, too, and meaningful occupation in the patient working out of rhyme and pentameter, image and the system of correspondences by which the classical divisions were understood to be linked: springtime with childhood, winter with old age, fire with choler, earth with melancholy, and so forth. But the twentieth-century interlocutor Berryman invents will have none of it:

> To please your wintry father? all this bald
> abstract didactic rime I read appalled . . .
>
> (*Ibid*)

Anne Bradstreet Now. Abram Van Engen and Mary Eyring, Oxford University Press.
 DOI: 10.1093/9780197811191.003.0012

Berryman is not the only reader to have dismissed Bradstreet's *Quaternions.* Adrienne Rich describes them as "long, rather listless,"[1] preferring the poems she can construe as arising directly from autobiographical "experience." But, in purely poetic terms, are lines like this, in which Bradstreet expresses fear for the life of her husband:

Thou hast relieved my fainting heart
Nor paid me after my desert;
Thou hast to shore him safely brought
For whom I Thee so oft besought.
("In Thankful Acknowledgment for the Letters I
Received from My Husband Out of England," 9–12)[2]

really so superior to lines like this from the *Quaternions*:

But wise Old Age did with all gravity
To childish Childhood give precendency,
And to the rest his reason mildly told,
That he was young before he grew so old.
("The Four Ages of Man," 53–56)

Or is it rather that the poems we can attribute to "personal experience" allow more scope for our own imaginative projection? "There were real parallels between her life and mine," writes Rich (xx), who has strong opinions about what women's poetry ought to be. As for Berryman, he complacently portrays Bradstreet's husband, like her father, as a figure inimical to her creative spirit, the better to offer himself, or the surrogate who speaks for him in "Mistress Bradstreet," as her truer soulmate:

I doubt if Simon than this blast, that sea,
spares from his rigour for your poetry
more. We are in each other's hands
who care. Both of our worlds unhanded us.
(Berryman, "Homage," 2)

[1] Adrienne Rich, Foreword, *The Works of Anne Bradstreet* (Cambridge: Harvard University Press, 2010), xv.

[2] For citations from Bradstreet's poetry, I have relied throughout on *Anne Bradstreet: The Works of Anne Bradstreet*, ed. Jeannine Hensley (Cambridge: Harvard University Press, 2010).

I have no intention of banishing sympathetic identification from our reading of Bradstreet's poetry; the ability to elicit such stirrings of imagination is one of her key powers. Still less do I intend to rank the relative excellence of her literary output. I would like, however, to become a better reader of her large-scale poems, which I confess I have been slow to warm to. And along the way, perhaps I'll be better able to account for the magic of moments that seem to me to detach from the orderly procession of the verse and startle us with their immediacy. As in the couplet cited above:

> And to the rest his reason mildly told,
> That he was young before he grew so old.

I'll return to this couplet again, but my overall argument will be the following: we needn't rely upon autobiography, or references to the poet's contemporary scenes and circumstances, in order to encounter the distinctively human voice in Bradstreet's poetry. That voice, in all its compelling power, is audible elsewhere, a touchstone for the mind and heart.

*

First, a confession. My resistance to Bradstreet begins with the rhymed couplet. I dislike the rhymed couplet. I consider it inimical to all that I hold most dear about poetic form: the play of syntactical and metrical resistance, the variable tempos of unfolding thought, the surprise of sudden concord in a field of impediment, the puzzle-work that keeps the poet just busy enough to be taken somewhere unexpected. The rhymed couplet is confining. It inclines toward the homiletic, the didactic, and the satiric (on that latter mode, see the long English eighteenth century). It is a form of packaging, a musical unit that too easily becomes a tidy unit of thought.

But what am I saying? Haven't I loved, don't I continue to love, the vitality of the couplet in Marvell:

> Had we but world enough and time,
> This coyness, lady, were no crime . . .
> ("To His Coy Mistress")

Aren't I endlessly amused by his effrontery and extravagance?

I would
Love you ten years before the flood,
And you should, if you please, refuse
Till the conversion of the Jews.
(*Ibid*)

And aren't I a complete pushover when it comes to the capstone couplets in Shakespeare's sonnets:

For thy sweet love remembered such wealth brings
That then I scorn to change my state with kings.
("Sonnet 29")

Yes, but. Case in point. Marvell uses the couplet against itself, against the ideals of Petrarchan love poetry, and against the imagined protestations of a reluctant mistress. Shakespeare wins through to his concluding couplets by way of quatrains notable for syntactical complexity and variable dynamics and, often as not, the supposed closure of those couplets is undermined by what has come before. Anne Bradstreet's more immediate model would have been the very different couplets of a poem we know she read devoutly: Joshua Sylvester's English translation of Guillaume Du Bartas' *La Sepmaine du Creation.* Du Bartas' epic poem had become a centerpiece of sixteenth- and seventeenth-century Puritan culture and is one of two models Bradstreet cites in the dedicatory epistle to the *Quaternions.* Her four-part sequence, like Du Bartas' *Seven Days of Creation*, as "Englished" by Sylvester, and like the other predecessor Bradstreet acknowledges (her father Thomas Dudley's "On the Four Parts of the World"), are narrative poems, whose expository obligations don't take kindly to the derailments and chronic subversions I tend to prefer. About Dudley's prosody we can only speculate, since his text has been lost to us. Sylvester, while faithful to clarity of outline, builds his couplets within the long arc and nested dependencies of hypotactic syntax. Here is a passage from the first day of creation:

Yet did this Nothing not at once receiue
Matter and Forme: For, as we may perceiue
That Hee who means to build a warlike Fleet,
Makes first prouision of all matter meet
(As Timber, Iron, Canuase, Cord, and Pitch)
And when all's ready; then appointeth, which

> Which peece for Planks, which plank shall line the waste,
> The Poup and Prow, which Fir shall make a Mast;
> As Art and Vse directeth, heedfully,
> His hand, his tool, his iudgement, and his eye:
> So God, before This Frame he fashioned . . . [3]

This gorgeous prosodic and syntactical syncopation is not what we encounter in Bradstreet's couplets. Far from it. So her distinctive play of mind and music must be of a different order. If I am to do them justice at all, I'll have to approach them from another angle.

*

One aspect of the *Quaternions* that comes more naturally to me as a reader is their embrace of allegory. I've spent a lot of time over the years with Spenser's *Faerie Queene* and have come to feel at home with the figurative propositions and cross purposes that allegory-set-in-motion entails. Bradstreet's allegory relies upon two primary literary tropes. The most conspicuous of these is allegorical personification: Fire, Earth, Water, Air, Choler, Blood, Melancholy, Phlegm, Childhood, Youth, the other Ages, and the Seasons are bodied forth in Bradstreet's poem as speaking personae. Second and equally foundational is the rhetorical mode of contestatory (or forensic) debate: the qualities and powers of Fire and Summer, Winter and Water are not neutrally rehearsed in the *Quaternions* but are marshalled as evidence in a contest over precedence. Fire adduces her powers over ripening, material transformation, and destruction too: "What famous towns to cinders have I turned?" ("Elements," 110). Earth claims foundational essence: "Remember sons, your mould is of my dust . . . / As Earth at first so into Earth returned" ("Elements," 262–264). Water, "angry" to have been so overlooked, goes on the attack: "Sister," she says to her sibling Earth, "This your neglect shows your ingratitude . . .

> But thou art bound to me above the rest,
> Who am thy drink, thy blood, thy sap and best:
> If I withhold, what art thou? dead dry lump,
> Thou bear'st no grass nor plant nor tree, nor stump.
> ("Elements," 270, 273–276)

[3] *Du Bartas His Deuine Weekes And Workes Translated: And Dedicated To The Kings Most Excellent Maiestie By Iosuah Syluester*, in the digital collection Early English Books Online (https://Name.Umdl.Umich.Edu/A11395.0001.001, University Of Michigan Library Digital Collections: Accessed September 5, 2024), DW, C4r.

In theory, an orderly allegorical scheme allows ample room for both narrative and figurative elaboration while preserving a clear foundation; personification and rhetorical debate infuse the whole with animated point of view. In practice, as Spenser's *Faerie Queene* so wonderfully illustrates, the orderly division of persons and perspectives tends to break down under the weight of its own representational contradictions. And this is the part that's especially good for poetry. Edmund Spenser held a central place in Europe's canon of Protestant poets and, like Sylvester's Du Bartas and Sir Philip Sidney, is among the authors specifically mentioned in Anne Bradstreet's written works. But we needn't posit extended acquaintance with Spenser's allegorical epic to account for commonalities in poems—the *Quaternions* and *The Faerie Queene*—that are in other respects so strikingly different from one another. Bradstreet had her own means of discovering the felicitous fault lines in the poetic scaffolding she chose for her first extended venture into poetry.

> The Fire, Earth, Air, and Water did contest
> Which was the strongest, noblest, and the best . . .
>
> ("Elements," 1–2)

But then they fall out before they have even begun, competing for supremacy in their speaking order:

> The quaking earth did groan, the sky looked black,
> The fire, the forced air, in sunder crack;
> The sea did threat the heavens, the heavens the earth,
> All looked like a chaos or new birth . . .
>
> ("Elements," 11–14)

And thus the poet reminds us of the material realities behind the distillations of poetic figuration. Metaphoric vehicle unveils its naked tenor. Meanwhile, point of view is wonderfully composite. On the one hand, each self-promoting speaker advances her own case even to the point of comedy; on the other hand, the merely human perspective, the grounding, outside-the-fiction perspective, has a way of seeping in. Use value and human endeavor are central to each argument, as registered in the widening of address: "Ye martialists," says Fire, it is I who forge your instruments of war ("Elements,"

35ff). "Ye husband-men," she says, you would have no hoes or mattacks without my powers ("Elements," 44ff). Cooks, chemists, silversmiths: you are all dependent on me ("Elements," 50ff).

More accurate, perhaps, to refer to this phenomenon as *layered* point of view, an aptitude Bradstreet is happy to exploit. Take, for example, the figure of Choler from "The Four Humours": In Galenic physiology, choler, or yellow bile, was the bodily fluid thought to be hot and dry, most closely related to the element Fire and responsible, in excess, for the choleric, or quick to anger, temperament in human beings. "To show my high descent and pedigree" ("Humours," 30), says Choler, she conspicuously heightens the combative nature of debate and stakes her claim on the superiority of those who come under her influence:

> Have you not heard of worthies, demi-gods?
> Twixt them and others what is't makes the odds
> But valour? whence comes that? from none of you,
> Nay milksops, at such brunts you look but blue.
>
> ("Humours," 56–59)

Bradstreet's personae have sunk to *ad feminam* argument in the earlier "Elements" section too (see Water, above), but Choler intensifies that mode of attack, and Bradstreet has great fun with it:

> Now let's give cold white sister Phlegm her right,
> So loving unto all, she scorns to fight . . .
> The brain she challengeth, the head's her seat;
> But know'ts a foolish brain that wanteth heat.
> My absence proves it plain, her wit then flies
> Out at her nose, or melteth in her eyes.
>
> ("Humours," 80–81, 104–107)

Here the wrapping-up potential of the end-stopped couplet is wickedly, and wittily, exploited to its full extent. Here we see the advantage of poetic syntax that fits so comfortably within the boundaries of a ten-beat line and a series of perfect, monosyllabic, rhyming downbeats. The allegorized nature of the Humours, like that of the Elements, invites us to imagine personae with capacious boundaries: concrete enough to be endowed with speaking voice and point of view, abstract enough to mobilize all the forms of learning known to humankind: scientific, philosophical, historical, geographic, botanical, musical, and more. But in a single stroke, one cunning insult can reduce an informing principle of nature to the merely human: a sniveling girl with a runny nose.

What are we to make, meanwhile, of Bradstreet's gender deployments? Choler and her fellow Humours are female, like the Elements and the Seasons, but her clinching argument for superiority is her ability to "make a man":

> And yet to make my greatness, still more great
> What differences, the sex, but only heat?
>
> ("Humours," 152–153)

(In Aristotelean physiology, the greater the heat at conception, the greater the chance that the resulting child will be male.) Bradstreet has professed her own inferior powers from the beginning of her enterprise: to her father, she describes her own "four times four" as "rudely penned" by a "humble hand" ("Dedication," 14, 18). She counts the usual stuff of epic as "too superior things" for "my mean pen" ("Prologue," 1). She describes her Muse as "foolish, broken, blemished" ("Prologue," 3). And, lest the gendered foundation of all this be unclear: "Men can do best, and women know it well" ("Prologue," 7). But the superb composure and masterful modulations of Bradstreet's verse argue otherwise. Here in her Prologue, the rhymed and end-paused lines of the poet's sestet are the perfect vehicle for her complex professions of humility. Such professions have a distinguished lineage after all, as readers of Edmund Spenser would know very well. Here is Bradstreet:

> And oh ye high flown quills that soar the skies,
> And ever with your prey still catch your praise,
> If e'er you deign these lowly lines your eyes,
> Give thyme or parsley wreath, I ask no bayes;
> This mean and unrefined ore of mine
> Will make your glist'ring gold but more to shine.
>
> ("Prologue," 8)

And so, returning to the Humours and to Choler, if using a female persona to confirm the incontestable superiority of men, via a learned argument from Aristotle, is not a case of simple irony, it is at least wittily destabilizing.

Gender assumes a heightened place in the third section of Bradstreet's poem. It is not merely in deference to a grammatical convention that Bradstreet makes her personae male in the "Four Ages of Man," but in tacit (and strategic) deference to an ideological premise as well: the gendered male is taken to be the exemplary human. This, as the unfolding narrative reveals, is not entirely to his advantage. Once again we see Bradstreet subjecting a commonplace to discomfiting entanglements. "The Four Ages" are anomalous in several respects. In this section, the poet all but abandons the rhetorical proposition that has lent so much momentum to her first two *Quaternions*: when the Ages begin to speak, it is not to argue but to show forth, to offer overview. And this showing-forth begins with the third-person prologue: as Childhood, Youth, "the Manly," and Old Age take their place upon the stage (and Bradstreet calls it a stage), they are described from an outside perspective, and more fully than has been the norm. For the first time, Bradstreet resorts to the Spenserian device of allegorical pageant, introducing the Ages according to their features, their emblematic adornments, and their "equipage" ("Ages," 51). Childhood wears a garland of "primrose, daisy and violet," the flowers of early spring, rides a hobby-horse, and carries "an hour-glass new begun" ("Ages," 16, 20); Youth wears "gorgeous attire" and a garland of midsummer blossoms, "roses, pinks and gilliflowers," and rides "No wooden horse, but one of mettle tried" ("Ages," 25, 29, 33). Manhood carries a sword, a basket of autumn fruits, and money in his purse ("Ages," 39–42), Old Age, a sheaf of wheat and a "glass even almost run" ("Ages," 47). Point of view has assumed a wider lens.

This becomes yet more conspicuous as the Ages begin to speak. Bradstreet's third quartet of speakers are personae with a difference: paradoxically, the categorical proximity of Childhood and any particular child, Manhood and any particular man, produces a succession of speakers less likely to exhibit the idiosyncrasies we associate with personality. In simple terms, the Ages are less like people than are the anthropomorphic figures of Fire, Earth, Choler, and Phlegm. The Humour Melancholy, for example, is an abstraction but she can speak with chilling condescension:

> I now speak unto all, no more to one,
> Pray here, admire, and learn instruction.
> My virtues yours surpass without compare . . .
> ("Humours," 453–455)

By contrast, the Ages appear to be lodged in something of a middle distance. Childlike interiority receives its due, for example, but no child ever spoke like this:

> My highborn soul so straitly was confin'd,
> That its own worth it did not know nor mind:
> This little house of flesh did spacious count,
> Through ignorance all troubles did surmount . . .
>
> ("Ages," 86–90)

The perspective is that of the speaker's later, "better" judgment, but this does not seem to me to capture either the full ambiguity of speaker position or the full resonance of the passage. "This little house of flesh" ("Ages," 88), like the apple and the plum ("Ages," 105) that constitute the objects of childish desire, speak with the same disarming simplicity as that which we encounter in Bradstreet's more explicitly autobiographical poems, in, for example, the humble "trunk" and "chest" that are part of her personal inventory in "Some Verses Upon the Burning of Our House" ("Burning," 29). All of the *Quaternion* personae are to double business bound: their poet is navigating a complicated representational realm, vibrating between two poles. And she is doing so with the same poignancy and deft economy we (rightly) celebrate in her more famous poems. We sense a speaker behind the speaker.

If Youth and Manhood speak with less poignancy on behalf of the self and those whose lives the self involves, it is perhaps because they have been charged with the task of speaking for a crowd, and a conspicuously heterogeneous crowd at that. Youth describes himself as all things to all men: learned, beautifully featured and attired, "[s]o affable, that I can suit each mind" ("Ages," 168), but also as dissolute, quarrelsome, vicious, and unrepentant about the damage he wreaks on self and others. His pronoun throughout is first-person singular, but the virtues and the vices, the pleasures and afflictions surveyed seem rather to belong to a sequence of alternative lives. This new fracturing of speaker position emerges with even greater clarity in Manhood, or "Middle Age." The premise seems to be that men in their maturity, in the fullness of temperament and vocation, can only be imagined in the aggregate if they are first acknowledged in their fullest differentiation. So Middle Age must speak in a series of conditionals:

> Be my condition mean, I then take pains
> My family to keep . . .
> If rich, I'm urged then to gather more . . .
> Was I a pastor, I my flock did feed . . .
> A soldier I, with speed I did obey . . .
> Was I a labourer, I wrought all day . . .
>
> ("Ages," 248–272)

One way of capturing the representational instability of Bradstreet's personae is to talk about *point of view*, a category I have found helpful. Another, which this portion of the *Quaternions* seems to require, is to ponder the concept of *acknowledgment*, the register that another life may be as real as one's own. It is striking, in this regard, to encounter the following passage in Childhood's speech:

> My mother's breeding sickness I will spare,
> Her nine months weary burthen not declare.
> To show her bearing pains, I should do wrong,
> To tell those pangs which can't be told by tongue:
> With tears into the world I did arrive;
> My mother still did waste as I did thrive.
>
> ("Ages," 64, 68–73)

Childhood has launched his section not with an interior perspective but with a biblical commonplace ("Ah me! conceived in sin and born with sorrow"), and his account is meant to be universal: that's the premise of allegory. But there is something more than overview in the lines about maternal suffering. The compassion evident in this passage encourages us to imagine specific human embodiment. Whose embodiment? Not that of an actual human child, who could neither speak this way nor know such things. Not that of the mother either, not exactly, but rather of one behind both figures who knows whereof she speaks.

As befits her faith and moral framework, Bradstreet is perfectly willing to condemn vice and praise virtue where she sees them. But when allegorical personification, and poetry more generally, become the vehicles for exploratory thought, any judgment the reader discerns and comes to feel is perforce both layered and refracted. Elements and Humours may hurl insults at one another and compete for prestige, but we are not encouraged to accuse water or blood of vanity; to do so would be to muddle tenor and vehicle. Occasionally, one voice emerges as more ameliorative, and thus more admirable, as in this speech by Phlegm:

> Let's now be friends; it's time our spite were spent,
> Lest we too late this rashness do repent . . .
> Two hot, two moist, two cold, two dry here be,
> A golden ring, the poesy UNITY.
>
> ("Humours," 596–604)

But much as we may warm to the sentiment, the moral in literal terms is no more than common sense: the bodily fluids require one another if they are to sustain life. And here lies one of the durable sources of liveliness in the *Quaternions*: as figure and ground divide the course of meaning between them, the reader is required to shuttle between two modes of understanding. If the distinction between figure and ground seems to blur sometimes or we are lulled into mistaking one for the other, well, that's when we become aware of the poet's suppleness, and of our own collaborative role in spinning out the fiction. Behind the antics and rhetorical embellishments of her personae, we are always aware of the poet's larger field of vision, her witty reservations of judgment, her compassion, and above all her acknowledgment of life beyond her own era and circumstance.

All the more striking, then, are the bizarre lapses in Manhood's disquisition on the life of agricultural labor:

> If to agriculture I was ordained,
> Great labours, sorrows, crosses I sustained. . . .
> If happiness my sordidness hath found,
> 'Twas in the crop of my manured ground,
> My thriving cattle and my new-milch-cow,
> My fleeced sheep, and fruitful farrowing sow:
> To greater things I never did aspire
> My dunghill thoughts or hopes could reach no higher.
>
> ("Ages," 282–293)

Heretofore, the litany of vices in "The Four Ages of Man" has focused on abuse of aptitude or circumstance. Childhood regrets his lapses into bad behavior: "Oft stubborn, peevish, sullen, pout and cry" ("Ages," 128). Youth charges himself with squandering his gifts and education, reducing his parents to woefulness, and generally descending "From pipe to pot, from pot to words and blows" ("Ages," 193). But Manhood's self-portrait-as-agricultural-laborer appears to condemn a *way of life*. The thriving cattle and the new-milch-cow, the fleeced sheep and fruitful farrowing sow are granted a measure of poetic beauty, but what, in that context, are we to make of "sordidness" and "dunghill thoughts," especially when these qualities are said to be "mine"? I can only think of the moment as anomalous, as though the Bradstreet has failed for once to activate those subtle signs by which she habitually offers leverage on insufficient stereotypes. Representational instability is not always a source of augmentation.

Oddly, the only analogous moment I have found in the *Quaternions* occurs in "The Four Seasons," when Summer waxes lyrical about the pastoral way of life:

> Blest rustic swains, your pleasant quiet life,
> Hath envy bred in kings that were at strife,
> Careless of worldly wealth you sing and pipe,
> Whilst they're embroiled in wars and troubles rife . . .
>
> ("Seasons," 113–116)

This is straight out of Greek and Roman pastoral, which was always an urban fantasy. For Bradstreet, it's an odd concession to received attitude.

*

In "The Four Seasons," Bradstreet is released from the thornier representational terrain of "The Four Ages." No longer are her personae required by the awkward proximity of "Mankind" and actual human beings to be both one and many, exemplary and particular at once. The relative balance between abstraction and figurative representation is restored to what it was in the first and second *Quaternions*. And because the Seasons by their nature occur in annual rotation, one giving way to another which gives way to the next, this fourth *Quaternion* need not resume the dynamics of rhetorical debate which governed, albeit inconsistently, the Elements and Humours. "The Four Seasons" can relax into something more like a praise poem, and the poet into some of her most unfettered lyricism. Here is Spring:

> My second month is April, green and fair,
> Of longer days and a more temperate air . . .
> The primrose pale and azure violet
> Among the verdurous grass hath nature set,
> That when the Sun on's love (the earth) doth shine
> These might as lace set out her garment fine.
>
> ("Seasons," 44–55)

Less clement seasons may be less fulsomely celebrated—Winter may be "cold, moist [and] phlegmy"—but they escape the taunts and censure to which the Elements and Humours subjected one another. What sense would it make, after all, to moralize the seasons? The altered angle of approach has consequences for Bradstreet's versification as well. Freed from their polemical obligations, couplets in "The Seasons" are far less likely to slip into the didacticism that is at once the special power and the bane of rhyming end-stopped and end-paused couplets everywhere.

This is not to say that the poetry in the fourth of Bradstreet's *Quaternions* is rhetorically uninflected. How are we to take the following couplet on Winter's human toll, for example?

> Now toes and ears, and fingers often freeze,
> And travellers their noses sometimes leese.
>
> ("Seasons," 245–246)

I've been tempted to think of these lines as a moment of indulgent humor, the poet in a light-hearted moment using breezy summation to distance her verse from a reality that is anything but light. But have I heard mistakenly? The forced rhyme, or what I took to be a forced rhyme—freeze/leese—sounds slightly comic to me, but "leese" was a common alternative form of "lose" in Bradstreet's era. I'm hard pressed to detect a somber note in Bradstreet's abbreviated trot though the cold months (a mere twenty-seven lines to springtime's eighty-seven), but perhaps I have mistaken an orthographical feature for a register of tone.

I am on firmer ground in an earlier section of Winter's speech:

> Through Christendom with great festivity,
> Now's held (but guessed) for blest Nativity.
>
> ("Seasons," 237–238).

The moment is one of consummate poetic mastery: a world of learned skepticism summed up in two parenthetical syllables. Even as she honors the spirit of religious observation and human community, the poet makes clear she is no slave to mere convention. She has found space, without acerbity, to register her own independence of mind. Bradstreet has many bests, and this is one of them: the coincidence of elegant economy and sublime composure.

"I care not how the winter time doth haste" ("Seasons," 248), says Winter, and indeed, Bradstreet's poem appears to be hastening to its end. Not only is "Winter" the shortest of the Seasons, but his lines modulate, all but imperceptibly, into those that are avowedly those of the author. Here is the envoi to the whole:

My subject's bare, my brain is bad,
Or better lines you should have had:
The first fell in so naturally,
I knew now how to pass it by;
The last, though bad I could not mend,
Accept therefore of what is penned,
And all the faults that you shall spy
Shall at your feet for pardon cry.
("Seasons," 257–264)

I cannot agree with Bradstreet's own assessment of this, the last of her *Quaternions,* but the expedition with which she handles Winter, and the abruptness with which he is dismissed, convince me that she was well and truly ready to conclude her poem.

*

Time to return to the couplet that so captured my attention many readings ago and convinced me to listen more carefully to the tonal and figurative unfolding of Bradstreet's four quartets. We are back in the prologue to "The Four Ages of Man," when the question once again was which of the speakers ought to go first. Wise Old Age concedes the place to Childhood,

And to the rest his reason mildly told,
That he was young before he grew so old.
("Ages," 55–56)

Perfect pentameter, perfect rhyme, obedient monosyllables. The iambs lie down like lambs. The logic is simple: youth comes before age. But that is not what Old Age says. He makes it personal. He says that "*he* was young before he grew so old." Behind the screen of an allegorical persona and the abstraction for which he stands, we suddenly hear the voice of the simply human. This, to my mind, is Bradstreet at her most enchanting. And this most difficult accomplishment is one we always associate with her: achieved transparency. It is as luminous, I would argue, as anything to be found in her later poems.

Niki Herd

Meditations: A Remix

the town. thousands of enemies. one traitor within—

/

we see orchards. trees so fruitful. that is the breaking. some again. loaden. some nothing but leaves. so frequent in duties. bodies. estates. nothing to command. both cumber the ground—

/

innumerable objects enter. spacious room filled. most strange. an impossibility ever to be—

/

often stones. a thick air about them. full of contrition. black clouds. sweating effects—

/

spring after a long winter. the trees. that day when the sun appears. dry bones—

/

the words hold fast. put forward. should be master of assemblies. not only to, but also so that—

Anne Bradstreet Now. Abram Van Engen and Mary Eyring, Oxford University Press.
 DOI: 10.1093/9780197811191.003.0013

one sun. multitude of stars militant and triumphant. innumerable company. even in this life. obscure luster. from that. them shine so bright—

/

little world. little commonwealth. fixed and resolved. both accuser, excuser, witness, and judge. the evidence absolute. more to be accepted. there must be—

/

the peacock. his feathers spying black feet—

/

yellow leaves argue. gray hairs want little—

/

a good name. precious it is. good repute. good men. weighed and tried as the sentence—

/

nothing of admiration. the sons of men. so vast a disproportion. lump of loins. adam again. earth exceedingly beautiful. bones full of marrow. breasts of milk. the dead given all of this—

commentary:

formally, i was drawn to bradstreet's "meditations divine and moral" for its prose-like sensibility. the meditations aren't introspective in a traditional [lyrical] sense as much as they are moralistic and attempt to teach. this intention is fine but the desired outcome might be lost on the reader given the sheer number of "lessons" in the work. in thinking about language as materiality in a poem, where meaning may or may not exist, where there may be too little said or too much, i read through the meditations and chose several that lent themselves to reconfiguration. from those, i removed language [while maintaining the original order of the words] i found interesting from each in an attempt to create a new experience. i began with approximately twenty out of the original seventy-seven meditations—and "meditations: a remix" represents the twelve that remain. the experiment resulted in a poem new sentence-adjacent; a bare-bones, abstract take, that allows bradstreet's concern with morality to peek through, along with moments of levity—

Kimberly Johnson

Kind Reader

The most affordable, and most readily available, edition of Anne Bradstreet's work is the paperback volume edited by Jeannine Hensley. Published by an imprint of Harvard University Press, it has been continuously in print since its first appearance in 1967. It offers the modern reader, perhaps reluctant to pick up a 400-year-old collection of poetry, an inviting preface by Adrienne Rich, whose poetic and feminist *bona fides* lend—or lent, at the frothy curl of the second wave—a kind of revolutionary currency to these pages of intellectual, spiritual, and domestic reflection, From the volume's cover, a mostly grayscale sketch of a woman in a bonnet and dour puritanical collar (her lips and cheeks barely rouged with the pink of life) gazes with bold directness into the twenty-first century. This is not a portrait of Anne Bradstreet. Nor is the moony charcoal image of a besmocked and dutch-capped figure that decorates Bradstreet's page on the Academy of American Poets website a portrait of Anne Bradstreet.[1] Nor indeed does the near-hagiographic 1867 edition of *The Works of Anne Bradstreet*, published by Abram E. Cutter include a picture of the poet, though it does include a "portrait, on India paper, of her husband, Governor Bradstreet."[2]

*

The only picture available to us of Anne Bradstreet is, I suppose, the one that endures through her words. But words offer a tricky bit of portraiture—for any poet, given the ways that a poem resists efforts to fix it to the actual life of its author. Even beyond such common obstacles, in the case of Bradstreet, there are so many mediations between the poet and her twenty-first-century reader, so many claims made about her, on behalf of her, for her, in her own time and in the centuries since, that if a reader wishes for some kind of view

[1] https://poets.org/poet/anne-bradstreet.

[2] For an account of Cutter's efforts to celebrate this earliest of American poets, including details about the images he includes, see Patricia Pender, "Constructing a Canonical Colonial Poet: Abram E. Cutter's *Bradstreetiana* and the 1867 *Works*," in *PBSA* 109.2 (2015), 223–246.

Anne Bradstreet Now. Abram Van Engen and Mary Eyring, Oxford University Press.
 DOI: 10.1093/9780197811191.003.0014

of the woman to whom the poems are attributed, it's hard to know where to look. Indeed, in her poems as in the portrait that Cutter includes in his edition, the image of Bradstreet gets refracted through those with whom she is in some kind of relation: husband, father, brother-in-law, children.

*

According, at least, to the explanation with which the book begins, Bradstreet seems not to have been involved in the publication of *The Tenth Muse*, the volume that introduced her poems to a reading public. The good Reverend John Woodbridge, Bradstreet's brother-in-law through her sister Mercy Dudley, had carried a manuscript of Bradstreet's poetry back to England with him after having spent time among the Dudleys in the Massachusetts colony. In his prefatory remarks to the "Kind Reader," Woodbridge writes, "I feare the displeasure of no person in the publishing of these Poems but the Authors, without whose knowledge, and contrary to her expectation, I have presumed to bring to publick view what she resolved should never in such a manner see the Sun."[3] This narrative is now a familiar episode in Bradstreet lore: the poems displayed to the common eye without Bradstreet's awareness or permission, the poet piously shielded from the sullied business of publication not only by her colonial distance but also by her unknowing.

*

I am struck not only by Woodbridge's canny protestations about Bradstreet's demure writerly reserve but also by his addressing the reader, the very "publick view" that he acknowledges might impugn Bradstreet's modesty, as "Kind."

> "Old Saxon *-kund*, Old High German *-chund*, *-chunt*, Old Icelandic *-kundr*, Gothic *-kunds*, suffix forming adjectives with the sense 'of the nature of' < a suffixed form of the Germanic base of kin *n.1*."[4]

*

[3] Bradstreet, *The Tenth Muse Lately sprung up in America. Or Severall Poems, compiled with great variety of VVit and Learning, full of delight. Wherein especially is contained a compleat discourse and description of The Four Elements, Constitutions, Ages of Man, Seasons of the Year. Together with an Exact Epitomie of the Four Monarchies, viz. The Assyrian, Persian, Grecian, Roman. Also a dialogue between Old England and New, concerning the late troubles. With divers other pleasant and serious Poems. By a Gentlewoman in those parts* (London: Stephen Bowtell at the signe of the Bible in Popes Head-Alley, 1650), A3v.

[4] https://www.oed.com/dictionary/kind_n?tab=etymology#40179503.

Which is to say: Woodbridge's introduction of poems that engage, remarkably, philosophy, natural history, politics, and the Classics, invites the reader to view the poet as familiar, as *familial.* As kin.

*

How forcefully our experience of Bradstreet's poetic corpus is scaffolded by family, by the ways that she is *in relation to.* Bradstreet's first poem in *The Tenth Muse* is the dedication "To her most Honoured Father *Thomas Dudley* Esq; these humbly presented" (B1r). Bradstreet signs this dedicatory verse as if it were personal correspondence: "From her, that to your selfe more duty owes, / Then waters, in the boundlesse Ocean flowes" (43–44). Following the poem in bold majuscule, a declaration of authorship, of authority, stealing in under the semblance of a devoted daughter's signature: ANNE BRADSTREET.

So too does she subscribe herself at the conclusion of her poem "The four Seasons of the Yeare": "Your dutiful Daughter. A. B" (64).

*

In introducing Bradstreet's poems, which in *The Tenth Muse* evidence the poet's ready facility with an impressive catalogue of literary and scientific disciplines, Woodbridge praises not her voracious compounding of different fields of study in her verses but her "discreet managing of her family occasions."[5]

*

The second edition of Bradstreet's work, published posthumously in Boston in 1679 under the title *Several Poems*, invites us further into familiar, or familial, relation to the poet. This expanded volume includes a number of more personal writings, whose titles encourage us to imagine Bradstreet even more firmly within a set of relational ties:

> "A Letter to her Husband, absente upon Publick employment."
> "Another."
> "Another."
> "To her Father with some verses."
> "In reference to her Children, 23. June, 1659."
> "In memory of my dear grand-child Anne Bradstreet. Who deceased June 20, 1669. being three years and seven Moneths old."[6]

*

[5] *The Tenth Muse*, A3v.

[6] Titles from *Several Poems Compiled with great variety of Wit and Learning, full of Delight; Wherein especially is contained a compleat Discourse, and Description of The Four Elements,*

Despite the assertions of its title page—"The second Edition, Corrected by the Author, and enlarged by an Addition of several other Poems found amongst her Papers after her Death"—Bradstreet seems not to have been involved in the publication of *Several Poems* any more than she was in *The Tenth Muse.* About *Several Poems*'s claims of authorial participation, Margaret Thickstun notes that "Beyond its possible marketing value, we have no documentation of what 'corrected by the author' actually means, and the internal evidence for a complete and intentional revised copy text is not compelling." Thickstun concludes, "There is no external evidence that Bradstreet anticipated or desired republication in print."[7]

Several Poems explicitly admits that it includes material that Bradstreet did not intend for print. The section of material added since the publication of *The Tenth Muse* in 1650—mostly poems addressing family members and domestic events—is preceded by a subtitle: "Several other Poems made by the Author upon Diverse Occasions, were found among her Papers after her Death, which she never meant should come to publick view, amongst which, these following (at the desire of some friends that knew her well) are here inserted."[8]

*

Adrienne Rich describes the expansions of *Several Poems* this way: "No more Ages of Man, no more, Assyrian monarchs; but poems in response to the simple events in a woman's life: a fit of sickness; her son's departure for England; the arrival of letters from her absent husband . . ."[9] I think Rich means to praise Bradstreet, but to my mind *the simple events in a woman's life* savors more of condescension than celebration.

*

In "The Author to her Book," one of the poems that appears for the first time in *Several Poems*, Bradstreet laments the publication of her work, addressing

Constitutions, Ages of Man, Seasons of the Year, Together with an exact Epitome of the three first Monarchyes, Viz, The Assyrian, Persian, Grecian, and Beginning of the Romnane Common-wealth to the end of their last King: With diverse other pleasant & serious Poems, by a Gentlewoman in New-England. The second Edition, Corrected by the Author and enlarged by an Addition of several other Poems found amongst her Papers after her Death (Boston: John Foster, 1679).

[7] Margaret Olofson Thickstun, "Contextualizing Anne Bradstreet's Literary Remains: Why We Need a New Edition of the Poems," in *Early American Literature* 52.2 (2017): 409–410.

[8] *Several Poems*, 237.

[9] Adrienne Rich, "Anne Bradstreet and Her Poetry," Foreword to *The Works of Anne Bradstreet*, edited by Jeannine Hensley (Cambridge: Belknap Press, 2010), xvii.

her verses directly and warning them away from inhospitable readers, "Vulgars" and "Criticks" (19-20). We should perhaps not be surprised that the figure she chooses to describe her book is familial: "Thou ill-form'd offspring of my feeble brain" (1), "My rambling brat (in print)" (8). Despite her ostentatious cataloguing of its blushing shortcomings, Bradstreet is nevertheless its "mother" (8), and "yet being mine own, at length affection" motivates her sense of protection toward it (11). Her book is a homely thing, dressed in "home-spun Cloth" (18), which "after birth did'st by my side remain" (2). Indeed, the crisis only arises when her poetic offspring is "snatcht from thence by friends, less wise then true / Who thee abroad, expos'd to publick view" (3–4). Bradstreet's poems are household creatures, imperiled when they leave the hearth of her care.

By describing her book as her child, Bradstreet ensures that we encounter her primarily through a figure that emphasizes maternal nurture. Even as we approach Bradstreet by reading words on a page in a book, she gently invites us to enter into relation to her as a mother.

*

Bradstreet seemed to believe that the medium of language might be sufficient to preserve something of its author—or at least this is the substance of a brief verse affixed like an epigraph to pages in the Andover Manuscript, a set of writings addressed explicitly to her most intimate circle:

To my dear children.

This Book by Any yet vnread,
I leaue for yov when I am dead,
That being gone, here yov may find
What was yr liueing mothers mind.

Here is Bradstreet's very "mind," an intimacy offered to her dearest readers as a legacy, the words a lively substitute for "yr liueing mother" even after her death. The careful ink, angular and firm as faith upon the fragile parchment, lineaments a spirit long after its fleshy husk turned to puritan dust in the New England soil.

Should it matter to me, then, that this slight and tender dedication appears in the Andover Manuscript not in Anne Bradstreet's hand, but in her son Simon's?[10]

*

As I consider how firmly Bradstreet's legacy is bound to her familial relations, I think of the matter that comprises the bulk of both *The Tenth Muse* and *Several Poems.* As the giddy full titles of these books attest, their pages are dominated by the quaternions, long and rhetorically complex poems that incorporate learning across a wide range of subjects. Bradstreet's quaternions synthesize knowledge about astronomy, geography, medicine, agriculture, meteorology, history, Classical and contemporary literature, politics, and the Bible. They are the product of robust education and stunning intellectual ambition.[11]

The Norton Anthology of Poetry's selection of Bradstreet's poetry includes her elegy for Queen Elizabeth and six domestic poems. And none of the quaternions.

The Norton Anthology of American Literature includes "Contemplations" and eleven familial poems. And none of the quaternions.

The Broadview Anthology of American Literature does include a brief selection from one of Bradstreet's quaternions, "The Four Monarchies," and it includes her "Meditations Divine and Moral." And also seventeen familial poems.

*

all this bald
abstract didactic rime I read appalled

—John Berryman, "Homage to Mistress Bradstreet," 93-94

*

[10] The most exhaustive catalogue of textual sources for Bradstreet's poems can be found in the editorial apparatus of *The Complete Works of Anne Bradstreet*, ed. Joseph R. McElrath, Jr. and Allan P. Robb (Boston: Twayne Publishers, 1981). The brief dedicatory verse appears on page 215 of that volume.

[11] For an assessment of the logical structure of the quaternions and the strands of learning that gave rise to them, see Jane Donahue Eberwein, "The 'Unrefined Ore' of Anne Bradstreet's Quaternions," in *Early American Literature* 9 (1974): 19–26. For the argument that the quaternions reflect the

the simple events in a woman's life

*

It *does* matter to me that the intimate dedication to her children is in Simon's hand. Although it doesn't occur to me to feel this way about other poets, precisely because Bradstreet's work is so bound to familial ties, both thematically and in the narrative of its presentation to the world, I find that I'm desperate to find a Bradstreet that is not *in relation* to—that is not mediated by the authorizing presence of another. I want her nimble and voracious mind unsubject to the seemliness of her status as *a Gentlewoman in New-England.* I want her poems not as her brother-in-law determines, not as her honored father may approve. I want her to flex her own authority without modesty or apology. I want a Bradstreet not curated for me by parent, in-law, husband, children, grandchildren, John Berryman, Adrienne Rich.

I don't want to be a kind reader of Bradstreet. I want to be a provoked, stymied, excited, and even estranged reader. I don't want Bradstreet to be my mom; I want her to be my challenger.

*

Given all Bradstreet's admirable learning, her wide and precocious reading, her observational experience, and her industry, it bothers me most deeply that I, too, like her domestic poems best.

*

Amidst pages of material in her son Simon's hand, much of it transcribing Bradstreet's holographic prose and poetry from a source no longer extant, the Andover Manuscript contains some pages of text in Anne's own handwriting. Those pages preserve not only Bradstreet's work but her revisions of her work, providing a record of the process of her thinking and rethinking. If I copy here some of the text in her hand along the left margin, and include the editors' notes about the material artifact of the manuscript in another column to the right, it begins to seem to me a kind of poem—briefer than the poems published in her two seventeenth-century volumes, to be sure, and less constrained by the couplets she favored, but suggesting nevertheless something of the yearnings, fears, and prayers that drove Bradstreet to write. Something about unease and hope, urgency and contemplation, solitude and social value.

seventeenth-century domestication of women's education, see Robert Hilliker, "Engendering Identity: The Discourse of Familial Education in Anne Bradstreet and Marie de l'Incarnation" in *Early American Literature* 42.3 (2007): 435–470; and Elizabeth Ferszt, "Transatlantic Dame School: The Early Poems of Anne Bradstreet as Pedagogy," in *Women's Studies* 43.3 (2014): 305–317.

nothing more	What appears a comma follows "more." It is judged the effect of nonauthorial scribbling (presumably by children) which occurs throughout Andover.
disquiet	"disquiet" was first written with a malformed "ui," then it was canceled and rewritten to the right.
ouer throw	"ouer throw" appears above a canceled "destroy."
filled	Following "filled" is a canceled "neuer."
desireing	There was a hole in the manuscript book p. 23 at the time that Bradstreet wrote Meditation 53: thus we find "desire" on p. 23 and the "ing" ending written through the hole, onto p. 25.
price	Following "& wthout" appears a caret with "price" above it.
good	"good" was originally "god"; the *d* was made to resemble an *o* and *d* was added.[12]

*

here yov may find
What was yr liueing mothers mind.

*

Kind Reader, I do not presume to speak for Bradstreet about what these revisions, in aggregate, mean. I do not presume to know this woman. But I do know the urge that spurs revision—the false starts and vague linguistic doodlings, the black lines that strike an infelicity from the page with a force that sometimes tears the paper, the impatient scratch that records the violent transubstantiation of one word into another, of one thought into another. All the material traces of hard and solitary thinking. That urge is not *in relation to* anything but the poem. It's a kind of grief that has nothing to do with sickness or loss or the burning of a homestead but rather the pressure of relentless labor toward an ideal that exists nowhere but in the poet's own aspiration. These inky signs of Bradstreet's poetic process are not demure nor modest nor gentle nor kind but fierce and singular.

Woodbridge can claim the mother in what words were made public; I claim the truest picture of the poet in what was, finally, left out.

[12] The material in Bradstreet's handwriting in the Andover Manuscript is reproduced in McElrath and Robb, eds., *The Complete Works of Anne Bradstreet*, 260–265. The editors of that edition explain that in reproducing the matter in Anne Bradstreet's hand, they have preserved the messy idiosyncrasies of her style "without editorial regularization," imagining the reader of their edition to "want to know what Anne actually wrote, not what we could emend it to" (xxxv).

John Keene

Centos (for Anne Bradstreet)

after John Berryman and Naoshi Aguirre

B	I	C	O	N	T	E	S	T	E	M	O	C	Y	L	D	N	U	O	S
Y	N	A	N	W	D	K	F	H	R	D	G	L	O	R	Y	I	N	G	K
H	T	S	O	O	O	E	C	I	O	J	E	R	T	W	H	E	N	W	Y
S	E	T	T	H	G	I	N	S	C	A	P	T	A	I	N	S	C	L	T
V	N	H	T	S	L	E	P	T	B	B	T	R	I	V	S	T	I	W	N
L	T	O	J	E	H	A	T	H	E	H	S	J	R	N	U	A	G	E	O
U	X	U	B	W	R	M	G	D	G	R	G	U	B	V	D	I	D	W	T
F	I	R	E	A	A	C	N	N	U	N	S	O	O	N	E	R	Y	M	P
K	S	E	H	T	D	U	E	O	N	E	O	T	H	E	R	S	O	U	M
N	R	V	E	E	O	P	F	S	Z	K	U	X	A	Z	Y	A	R	S	A
A	A	O	A	R	Z	T	L	N	F	A	L	L	N	B	N	I	E	E	H
H	E	D	D	S	R	E	I	E	U	G	N	O	T	H	T	H	C	J	T
T	L	N	Q	A	E	G	Y	N	Q	O	F	L	C	V	H	A	A	T	R
H	E	A	R	P	H	L	W	K	D	N	D	L	N	X	S	P	L	K	O
Z	Q	H	N	T	H	O	P	G	A	E	O	A	T	L	W	P	P	A	N
S	M	T	L	D	E	F	B	N	I	W	O	T	H	V	O	Y	U	H	S
L	G	R	S	W	G	M	D	U	P	Q	T	E	P	T	R	I	G	E	B
A	D	O	E	O	T	H	E	R	S	H	S	L	G	Z	R	N	K	L	X
I	S	N	A	M	O	N	G	P	A	Y	Bd	Y	C	N	O	N	C	E	M
N	A	M	O	W	D	E	H	S	I	L	B	U	P	T	S	R	I	F	O

Then water in the boundless ocean flows will you make glist'ring gold, but more to shine but dare not go
beyond my Element and God shall blesse you from above and love him to Eternity praises to him Aye and
then with thee which is the best then I may fruitfull bee me lasting life shall give Till I dissolved bee And at
the most a simple mite that flegm was judg'd for kindness to excel for ever happefy'd with Thee for of
thine Almes I live but graunted hath my Suit oure vpright walking may expresse shee loues thee all thy
Dayes all Praises vnto Thee return Thee what I owe and so desire ev'n all my Dayes in strict and vpright
ways my hope and Treasure lyes Above then Come deare bridgrome Come away and in that hope I bid
you all farewell Shall at your feet for pardon cry and now the *Persian* Monarchy began him to the grave
did Traitor *Bessus* send *Ne sutor ultra crepidum* may write and people swear he'r to accept of King hath
many Ages been upon his knees and in a while, you'le tell another tale.his bones do lie interr'd in stately
Pauls that *Sidney* dy'd 'mong most renown'd of men *But Fame out-living both, he is reviv'd Eliza* shall rule
Albion once again *the greater was our gain, our loss the more in every one be her great glory fam'd* and
warlike weapons perished away *if some rejoyc'd, more did lament* then dying, left a blessed memory shall
last and shine when all of these are gone take thou the world, and all that will and all the rest, but Vanity
we find which caus'd her thus to send thee out of door the foule belongs to thee and brought me to the
shore from troubled Main who with salt tears this last Farewel did take I here, thou there, yet both but one
that when we live no more, we may live ever by all our loves conjure him not to stay at home, abroad, and
every where yet paying is not payd until I dye I happy am, if well with you is by his hand alone that guides
nature and fate thou with thy Saviour art in endless bliss among the blest in endless joyes remain he

Anne Bradstreet Now. Abram Van Engen and Mary Eyring, Oxford University Press.
 DOI: 10.1093/9780197811191.003.0015

"Cento (for Anne Bradstreet)" by John Keene

This poem comprises a series of centos, or a poem culled from individual words, phrases, and lines in a preexisting text or texts, here from Anne Bradstreet's own poems, and, more specifically, from the opening lines of some of her best-known poems. It takes the form of a (crossword) puzzle in order to mirror my attempts to understand, by reading and puzzling line by line and word by word, through her poetry in the context of her day and our own. The puzzle's hidden words not only can spell out her opening lines but also can spur the creation of new ones drawn from her language and ideas, from her era in conversation with our own. The words' and lines' initial concealed quality also might suggest the possibility of creating new poems created from her words as well as unearthing and revealing new meanings from her poems and newly created ones. This cento also takes the form of a palimpsest, with the final lines of nearly all of Bradstreet's poems in *The Works of Anne Bradstreet in Prose and Verse,* edited by John Harvard Ellis (Gloucester, 1962) hovering, in grayed out, phantasmal fashion, behind the primary puzzle poem, to form a second cento text in conversation with the primary one. Viewing this second text closely, if that is possible, the reader can see and hear Bradstreet's words—her voice, her poetry—directly, yet nevertheless transformed by this puzzle's form and spatiality, into a new poem, or multiple poems, opening up continuous new possibilities for reading and understanding the work and words of this vital American poetic pioneer.

Karen An-hwei Lee

Responsive Odes to Anne and her Microcosmos

The gray rock wasn't large, although it was famous. In fact, to my recollection, this rock I visited on field trips as a girl growing up in Massachusetts was an ordinary one, and did not stand out, at least, to the uninformed eye. It wasn't buffed and smooth like the glass stone my playmate picked up on our school playground, the size of a plum pit. It was much smaller than the granite boulders in the quarries, or the various boardwalks and piers on the Cape. It would not stand out among other renowned rocks that would comprise my topographical memory—the proud turtle rock of an eponymous residential neighborhood in Irvine, California; the ballast boulders of the landfill peninsula called Shelter Island in San Diego; or the porous dolostone on the façade of the campus building where I work today, dolostones which—during the last renovation—were made into paper weights and keepsakes.

Our overseas relatives, mostly my aunties, murmured when we took them Plymouth to see this ordinary, weathered rock—and they were perplexed not only by the stone itself, despite the notion that it bore the aura of history, but how gray it all was—the clapboard houses, the dirt roads, and the cisterns. The aunties from the motherland, Taiwan, who were baffled, asked—why are you taking us to see these shacks and houses without running water, and this gray rock? Centuries ago, our ancestors also left a motherland province for a new life, although not for the cause of religious freedom, but due to famine, according to my parents; they settled across the strait in Taiwan, and like the Plymouth brethren, encountered Austronesian indigenous people; the *Gaoshan* people—transliterated, High or Tall Mountain—are a marginalized population in Taiwan to this very day. My aunties, however, were not impressed by the pilgrim settlement with its cooking fires, dried maize, and cracker biscuits called hard tack.

Anne Bradstreet Now. Abram Van Engen and Mary Eyring, Oxford University Press.
 DOI: 10.1093/9780197811191.003.0016

Anne Bradstreet did not disembark on this rock as the Mayflower pilgrims did, although a rugged coastline of gray rocks would've greeted her in Salem's rugged coastline, north of today's Cape Cod and south of Cape Ann.[1] These stones and rocks would later figure in her poems, such as "Contemplations," a natural part of the terrain where she made her home with Simon, her colonial magistrate husband, in the New World.[2] Bradstreet crossed the sea not on the Mayflower but the slightly lesser-known Arbella, which made its mark in history by bearing passengers such as John Winthrop, who delivered "A Model of Christian Charity" in England before they boarded the ship during its crossing; the Arbella also carried a precious copy of the charter for the Massachusetts Bay Colony, where Winthrop would serve as governor. The Arbella was one of many ships in the Winthrop Fleet that departed from Northampton and landed in Salem.[3]

About three centuries later, in the decade of the Sixties, my parents would cross the ocean from Taiwan by airplane, not by ship; their weathered, gray rock would be their disembarkment in Seattle and Los Angeles, then in Chicago, respectively, eventually settling outside Boston, Massachusetts, not far from the places where Anne Bradstreet lived and wrote. For the first years of my life, I was unaware that this early American woman writer, in fact, dwelled in our family home in the form of anthologized poems. In my mind's eye, I associate Anne Bradstreet not as much with her pilgrim peers in Massachusetts Bay Colony, but with the portal holes in a small pocket anthology which prior owners left behind in the house where my family lived. It was the first volume of a two-volume set, each about the size of four silver dollars, and I could envision putting it in a large pocket and certainly a purse.

ANNE AND HER MICROCOSMOS

Dear Anne, the pocket anthology
is only big as four silver dollars,
about the size of a paperweight
or a coin purse. In these pages,

[1] "Anne Bradstreet, 1612–1672," *The Poetry Foundation*. https://www.poetryfoundation.org/poets/anne-bradstreet.

[2] "Anne Bradstreet, 1612–1672," *The Academy of American Poets*. https://poets.org/poet/anne-bradstreet.

[3] "Anne Bradstreet," *The New World Encyclopedia*. https://www.newworldencyclopedia.org/entry/Anne_Bradstreet.

I first encountered your verse—
your diction older than Elinor,
Marianne, Elizabeth, Emily,
less modern than Ruth

and Muriel. You had no face
and barely a biography—
only your lines on flesh
and spirit, to Simon,

and the burning
of your house
seared into
memory's

micrographs
of the brainy
cosmos you
embodied.

In my twenties, I watched an interview between Sharon Olds and Michael Silverblatt, a literary event sponsored by the Lannan Foundation.[4] During the interview, Sharon Olds referred to an edition of an anthology with "portholes." As a girl, she had a dream of one day seeing her own portrait in one of the portholes. My recollection from girlhood is that Anne Bradstreet was not one of a few women featured in the aforesaid portholes, although she was included in the anthology—alongside Elizabeth Bishop, Emily Dickinson, Marianne Moore, Muriel Rukeyser, Ruth Stone, Elinor Wylie (whose "Velvet Shoes" we took as dictation in an elementary school class for language arts), and a lesser known female poet by the name of Gene Derwood, whom I would later learn was the editor's wife—the anthology editor himself, none other than the poet Oscar Williams.

Anne Bradstreet's face was not framed in a porthole; rather, she was blank—no countenance at all—yet her poems spoke boldly and bodily, and she fully present despite her featurelessness. There was no porthole portrait of Anne Bradstreet because no image of her was made during her lifetime, at

[4] Sharon Olds, interview by Michael Silverblatt, *Readings and Conversations, the Lannan Foundation.* 10 April 2002. https://lannan.org/media/sharon-olds-with-michael-silverblatt.

least, not one that the anthologists and literary scholars were aware existed; no paintings or portrait miniatures, neither sketches nor silhouettes, and the daguerreotype had yet to be invented. In later years, I would realize a number of women poets were not included, such as Hilda Doolittle, Adrienne Rich, Sara Teasdale, and Phillis Wheatley, among many others who did not appear in the portholes of this early pocket edition published by Washington Square Press in 1955. It sold for seventy-five cents. I imagine the sea crossing she made with Simon as a member of the Winthrop Fleet—and wonder what she looked like, as well as whether the Arbella had any portholes which framed her face as she looked at the waves.

THE MISSING PORTRAITS OF ANNE

Anne, we don't know what you looked like.
Your face is missing among the portholes

on the anthology, four silver dollars wide—
there are no cameo silhouettes of you,

no thumbnail sketches or paintings,
not even a miniature of your head.

Your verse is your countenance—
every line a tilt of your nose

or lift of your chin, a hand
upon your aching forehead

as your rhymed stanzas glow
with fevered inspiration.

Maybe your portraits
were just too small—

kindred cosmos
of the humours.

THE SEA CROSSING

I cannot fathom what it was like to survive
in the dark hold of a ship named *Arbella*
with other pilgrims whose fastidiousness
alone would make me turn my back

to the New World, to New England.
You survived, Anne. You stood by Simon
and set up house in the bay colony,
living out your faith in God the way

we might go to the moon nowadays.
Yours was a brave religious frontier—
I cannot imagine an Atlantic storm
so fierce that the sails could take
the mast down in the wind. The sea

is your rite of passage, your hyphen
of monarchy and new democracy
you would not live to see, I'm sure
you'd be called a firecracker today.

As I revisit the "Model of Christian Charity" delivered by John Winthrop, I am struck by his call to unity and charity as a body politic, first and foremost as the body of Christ, not to be fractious or fractured by discord: "We must delight in each other; make other's conditions our own; rejoice together, mourn together, labor and suffer together, always having before our eyes our commission and community in the work, as members of the same body. So shall we keep the unity of the spirit in the bond of peace."[5] On hindsight, and in a social context of polarization, this vision of a "city on a hill" is a harbinger of American exceptionalism—the underlying assumption of supreme difference from other nations, and set apart for a purpose—a tiny but mighty seed of superiority in our nation's forbears, if not foreboding about the type of fruit it would bear in due time. I think of the parable of the large mustard tree in Matthew 13:31–32 where all the birds come to roost. In this

[5] John Winthrop, "A Model of Christian Charity," *Internet Archive.* https://archive.org/stream/AModelOfChristianCharity/AModelOfChristianCharity_djvu.txt.

parable, the Kingdom of Christ starts with faith the size of a mustard seed only a little larger than the dot at the end of this sentence. What if the parable of the mustard seed were figuratively transposed to a political nation and body politic, however, instead of a spiritual and heavenly kingdom? Isn't it this part of the nonconformist, Separatist seed which yielded both the firebrand abolitionists as well as the racist segregationists of the South?

As I reflect on what life was like for Anne Bradstreet—married at sixteen, a member of the Great Migration at eighteen in search of religious freedom away from persecution in England, and settling as a Separatist in the New World where she raised eight children; survived mysterious fevers, "brain-aches,"[6] and other ailments through the years; indulged in her poetry writing and prodigious interest in human anatomy and colonial medicine for various wounds, chronic pains, and the fatal consumption or tuberculosis, to which she succumbed; her intent reading of Helkiah Crooke's *Microcosmographia;* composed a heart-breaking poem to her beloved husband about her fear of death in childbirth ("Before the Birth of One of Her Children"); witnessed the burning of her house, an utterly devastating accident; and lived out her passion for God and her faithfulness to her church. Her sonorous diction with end-stopped rhymes, composed in the idiom of her era, showcases a rigor to her word-slinging ("physic-purging-potion" in line 15) in her unabashed criticism of "Popery" (line 215), and flaming critiques of Church of England and Roman Catholics. Her criticisms are riddled with references ranging from "Rome's whore, with all her trumpery" (line 237) to "tushes of the Boar" (line 44).[7]

ANNE, THE WORLD-SLINGER

Anne, you fearless word-slinger—
        if you took the stage at an open mike
in Los Angeles, a city of angels and drifters,
                        would Sunset Boulevard
glow with seraphs as the dazzling world
        dipped into the night? Would you wreck
its happy hours with searing messages
                        of salvation, the destiny

[6] Branka Arsić, "Brain-Ache: Anne Bradstreet on Sensing," *ELH* 80, No. 4 (Winter 2013): 1009–1043. https://www.jstor.org/stable/24475525.

[7] Anne Bradstreet, "A Dialogue Between Old England and New," *The Poetry Foundation*. https://www.poetryfoundation.org/poems/43700/a-dialogue-between-old-england-and-new.

of our Souls to utter doom if not for a Savior,
heralded by ancient prophecies?
You don't tell jokes—
no guffaws. Every inch an evangelist on fire,
the gospel unbridled, you go
to the end of the stage, you sling it—
you slay—Anne, a wordsmith extraordinaire—
Popery, ecclesial corruption,
the material excesses and bad clergy—
you leave no stone unturned
for the sake of Christ,
and your audience, mesmerized
by the fierce maze of linen and lace, gasps
as it applauds,
cut to the heart
by your act.

Structured metaphorically as a mother-daughter relationship, "A Dialogue Between Old England and New" personifies the motherland she left, England, and the New World as her daughter. If today's readers expect a postcolonial critique of the British Commonwealth from the vantage point of a new nation, far from it—Puritan public life, in which Anne Bradstreet and her colonial magistrate husband, Simon, were key influencers—did not harbor such decolonial sensibilities. Not at all a sea-crossing poem of immigration and diaspora rooted in a new world identity, where the ocean serves as a hyphenated cultural space and transnational geographical place of commerce, the dialogue's catechistic cadence and dogmatic impulse is a little too pat, tying its reassurances and conclusions with a rigid bow; as Bradstreet parses out a hopeful albeit an abbreviated pathway to resolving the tensions between the Church, monarchy, and Parliament, her last lines are, "Farewell, dear mother; Parliament, prevail, / And in a while you'll tell another tale" (lines 294–295).[8]

What today's readers might recognize as a more subversive than subservient gesture in this poem lies primarily in her criticism of the Church of England and the legal structures which enabled corruption in the clergy, personified through the pained and ailing mother, "Old England," and

[8] See Note 4 above.

the youthful daughter, "New England," who listens to her mother's woes and imparts a hopeful solace through a vision of healed and purified church: "Then Justice shall in all they Courts take place / Without respect of persons or of case. / Then bribes shall cease, and suits shall not stick long, / Patience and purse of Clients for to wrong . . . ./ So shall they happy Nation ever flourish, / When truth and righteousness they thus shall nourish" (lines 257-265).[9] If she were alive today, I wonder what Anne Bradstreet would think of the diversity of Protestant churches in North America, one on hand—juxtaposed to the Separatist ideals of the Puritans who came to the New World, on the other.

Today, as I revisit her most famous poems, I picture the street where Anne Bradstreet once lived with her husband, Simon, and their children before the house burned down. I imagine her moving thoughtfully in the domestic interior of her family and wisely navigating the public sphere of her colonial magistrate spouse. A privileged and educated, upper-class woman, she benefited from the support of household servants, even in the austerity of Massachusetts Bay Colony. I envision Anne Bradstreet's writing desk and her quill pen, the fine household objects and "pleasant things," as she referred to them, for a woman of her status in early colonial society—woman, wife, mother, and poet.

Additionally, I envision Anne Bradstreet speaking to her book in a prologue of misgivings and misapprehensions, a convention of her period, yet shot-through with the daunting imagery of the bodily suffering endured by women of the colonial era, such as birth defects, dire poverty, a range of female maladies, and fatal illness—without the benefits of modern medicine and the proper diagnosis of those ailments, compounded by an underlying social bias about women, which associated suffering with sin. A contemporary of another Anne—whose last name was Hutchinson, of the Anne Hutchinson controversy—she was most likely privy to the Antinomian Controversy and the public shaming and banishment of Hutchinson for her heterodox beliefs—a heterodoxy which was tragically blamed by misinformed theologians of the day for the "shapeless mass" she eventually birthed, as recounted by Jean Marie Lutes in "Theology and Gynecology: Anne Bradstreet's Representations of the Female Body."[10]

[9] See Note 4 above.

[10] Jean Marie Lutes, "Theology and Gynecology: Anne Bradstreet's Representations of the Female Body," *Signs* 22, No. 2 (Winter 1997): 309–340. https://www.jstor.org/stable/3175274.

THE STREET WHERE YOU ONCE LIVED

Dear Anne of the broad street, Bradstreet
of a Middle English dialect, of the stones
where you once lived in Salem, Ipswich,
Cambridge, Andover, not far the town

where I grew up, learning penmanship
as a daughter of immigrants; I wonder
whether you ever saw the Vynebrook
creek flowing near my house, milkweed

in meadow lakes of wild swans, a glow
in the marsh at night when small fireflies
and will-o'-the-wisp floated up the dark.
How did the names of our streets change

over the years, or did they ever change?
In your kitchen, you open the tea chest,
black tea from China for the colonies.
Your servants afforded you the time

to make your mark on the New World
with your lovely quarternions. Anne
of the broad street, of the Bradstreet
clan of patriarchal Puritan society,

will we ever see the unmarked grave
where you were laid to rest? No
image of you exists of your time,
not even a miniature.

THE BURNING OF YOUR HOUSE

Fire and fire she wrote, heart destroyed,
        dear Anne, all your worldly possessions
lying in a pile of ashes. *Beauty for ashes—*
        what in the world did a woman possess—
a silver salt shaker on a drop-leaf table,
        hairbrushes of wood or shell-bone,
a heart-shaped caddy spoon by a tea chest,
        a pomander orange studded with cloves,
objects you call *pleasant things in ashes.*
        Because all what we possess is mere ash,
I love the way you refer to money as *pelf—*
        to a modern ear, it rings of pelt and elf
or a mashed-up anagram of pilfer.
        Your clear, unclouded iambs, declare—
The world no longer let me love,
        My hope and treasure lies above,
your harmonious wordsmith's
        vowels booming like an organ
with all the stops pulled out
        if you had owned one, music
of pipes, valves, pedals praising
        God, whose fire purges us of vanities.

ANNE TALKS TO HER BOOK

Dear Anne, when you talk to your book,
is there a note of imposter syndrome,
or phenomenon, whatever we call it
these days? Why not fully embrace

your authorship as a woman with a brain
as well as a soul? I love the way you spell
critick as if it were a critical, literary cricket.
Let the *criticks* say whatever they want—

no one will remember their ceaseless
stridulation, their chirping, one-note
criticism, but the generations shall read
your poems, apostrophes of elisions

and contractions, and the archaic
stomp and splendor of your pen
spilling the cadence of your verse
onto a crisp, parchment page.

The words rise off the paper
like perfume, a fragrance
that your readers love—
your alabaster jar.

I ponder my aunts and cousins from the motherland of my parents, Taiwan, who visited Plymouth when I was a girl, and who were perplexed by the pomp and circumstance blessing the old settlement of "broken-down houses and bungalows," as they described it in the Taiwanese dialect. Plymouth itself has undergone a naming evolution from Plymouth Plantation—so identified when I visited as a girl in elementary school—to Plimoth Plantation as Governor William Bradford had called it, to a living museum renamed Plimoth Patuxet in honor of the indigenous people who lived in the region. Although my parents were immigrants under different circumstances—my father, an engineer, and my mother, a homemaker who would venture into her a career as an archivist after raising me and my little sister—they shared a hope that the "city on a hill," referred to as *Mei Guo* or the Beautiful Nation, would provide the type of freedom that the early colonists sought in their vision. It's this nascent republic and the pressures of assimilation that I consider in the girlhood context where I grew up, in Lexington, Massachusetts, the cradle of the American Revolution, the site of the Battle of Lexington, and one of the stops on Paul Revere's ride to warn the colonists of the British army's approach. It's the gestation of individualism and immigration I imagine as a sprig of hope in the green heart of the early colonists, Separatists willing to endure the severe hardships of the New World to live out their faith in God, and eventually, to found a nation based on democratic ideals—while inadvertently importing the vestiges of the Commonwealth which they wished to leave behind—into the future shining city of their new hopes and dreams.

ANNE, MY AUNTIES ARE PERPLEXED

Dear Anne, I apologize that my aunties
are underwhelmed—they 're unimpressed
by your Puritan life in this settlement,
the first published poet in the colonies

only a stone 's throw from Plymouth's
old village of broken bungalows—
my aunties gossip in their dialect.
Broken-down houses and bungalows,

small kitchens without running water,
gray dusks with a fear of the woods,
death from the smallpox and plague
without honoring the first people

who were there. Here. And in you,
the first seeds of Manifest Destiny,
mindless violence against the Other
with a so-called divine mandate.

My aunties do not spell out racism—
yet perhaps they see how this society
evolved from ideals that would mean
one day, my father, though trained

as an engineer, would spend hours
practicing a single word like *satellite*
in the basement of our home,
chanting it to syllabic perfection,

while forgetting whole sentences
in his heart-tongue and dialect,
and my mother would use Ming
as her name instead of the whole

transliteration. Ming, she'd say,
placing her hand over her heart,
as if saying a prayer or a pledge,
as easy to say as Anne—

a syllable in my Mandarin name,
a transliteration of peace, An—
although I'm not your namesake,
you are my forerunner in tongue.

In this final responsive ode to Anne Bradstreet, I reflect upon what it might've been like if Anne and I had been girlhood friends in a science fiction time travel episode where we meet each other on common ground, say, an apple orchard where my family would invite visiting relatives to pick the varieties—ones which may not have existed in her day.

ANNE IN THE APPLE ORCHARD

Dear Anne, what if we grew up
by the apple orchard where I
used to pick fruit with relatives
when they were visiting?

Did you ever go apple-picking,
I wonder? Surely fruit orchards
flourished among the Puritans,
or did you focus on gardening?

In Taiwan, the mountain-apples
and crisp apple-pears gleam
and glow like evening planets,
ripe poetry bound to nectar.

If we met in the lone orchard,
Anne, would you reach up, up
among the highest branches
to pick the sweet, gnarled

fall fruit, blossom-end first,
humming a favorite hymn?
And I'd take a few bushels
for buttery apple tarts

to share with your beau,
Simon. We'd talk until
sunset, and then more,
among the fireflies.

Shane McCrae

To Anne Bradstreet

Younger than Donne   and Herbert older than
Marvell   at least as more American
Than Edward Taylor exiled from the heart
As more for living there   with whom an art
Appeared   as first the sky with the first bird
Appeared   but as the mind with the first word
As more for living in the hearts of still
Americans who   any moment will
Remember they have hearts   and find you there
Anne Bradstreet you   who crossed the sea on air
As sure as sky is air   who rode across
The sea on top of the sea's sky   the loss
Of England was a mighty thing and bitter
And lost for what   for freedom   free bones litter
The chained Atlantic all   bound free in death
And died in your long wake both cow and calf
The meat and company both die together
As with the beasts by   which we live it ever
Has been   they die   and swim forever to
America   their souls belong to you
If creatures that do not have souls have souls
Or to the man whose name was on the rolls
Your father or your husband   but your father
Whichever name it was   it was a bother
-some business fleeing the king to embrace the King
In Massachusetts you found everything
Unclothed that had been dressed in streets and bricks
Houses that were not wishes   merely sticks

Anne Bradstreet Now. Abram Van Engen and Mary Eyring, Oxford University Press.
 DOI: 10.1093/9780197811191.003.0017

Your father doubtful of the English neighbors
The heaviness of the self-estranging labors
Of making a new home   how thoroughly
The labors changed you the   whales sailors see
In shadows in the waves dispel by breathing
Their homes into the air   but no more leaving
Or anyone who left would disappear
Entire   whereas in England everywhere
The streets the bricks as   if the people were
Expressions of the place and not its build
-ers and sustainers   everywhere was filled
With echoes of the people you had known
And who had left   and also now your own
Echoes though now   you couldn't hear them who then
Heard you   if when you spoke your voice fell through an
Abyss of trees   a horizontal cliff
The endless west to which you pledged your life

Before I wrote this poem, I hadn't engaged with Anne Bradstreet's work as much as I ought to have. Most of what I had read about her work indicated that, although it was historically important, as poetry it was second-rate. When I was asked to contribute something to this anthology, I recognized an opportunity to repair a deficiency in my knowledge about the history of poetry in America; soon after diving into her work and biography, I realized I had been gifted an opportunity to discover a new poet to love. Bradstreet's work surprised me with its strength and brilliance—in it, the heroic couplet re-discovers itself as a form not only for supple thinking, but also as a form for *beautiful* thinking, far-reaching thinking, renewing thinking. I tried, in my own poem, to respond both to Bradstreet's art and life in a form she would have recognized, and, in so doing, I discovered the form for myself. Surely rhyming couplets are underused nowadays because rhyming poetry is not now written as often as it once was. But just as surely, rhyming couplets are underused nowadays because they are difficult to write. More so than many other rhyming patterns, they pull the poet toward where *they* want to go, rather than toward where the poet wants to go. But that's also what makes them exciting. And it is exciting to encounter Bradstreet's own wrestling with the couplet, and to begin to come to grips with her achievement in it. She was the first great American poet, after whom we write, toward whom we write.

Anne Myles

Wrack

—contemplating Anne Bradstreet in another new world

I'm sitting in a deck chair somewhere close enough to the edge of the continent, thinking of you. Or trying to. It's not you who ever pulled me back across the centuries, to find a door that would open into the past—a wife and mother I could never be. Water shimmers crystalline in an above-ground pool. A bristly lawn runs across red dirt to an edge of woods. I haven't lived in North Carolina long, but it looks enough like where I came from that I can pretend my past isn't gone. A summer afternoon, familiar; like you I won't name too many species. Decades ago my cousin and I sat together on a dock by a lake in New York, and now we're both here. We remember things without having to say them. She has survived cancer for many years. We are in our bathing suits, icy tumblers slick in our hands. Sometimes this persistence feels like a miracle. Half-tame feral cats slink along the edges of the deck; she feeds and names them.

*

Let's say you're sitting with a quill in hand by the window of your house. The glass in diamond panes blurs present and memory for you too, brightness shimmering beyond the fractures. Let's make it high summer there as well—a trickle of sweat down your spine. That's the one thing I can be sure links us: what it feels like to exist inside a body. At this moment your old weakness and fainting are in remission, those *wasting pains which best my body knows*; you feel only the unthreatening grind of sit-bones on oak. You don't notice a finger tapping out iambics as you compose. You think of birds and fish, disporting themselves in bookish skies and streams. You think of the sun, rushing forward like an eager bridegroom. You think of your husband, aging perhaps but ruddy and strong, and of everyone else you love. Today, today.

Anne Bradstreet Now. Abram Van Engen and Mary Eyring, Oxford University Press.
 DOI: 10.1093/9780197811191.003.0018

Rapt were my senses at this delectable view. You can almost fill your lungs, almost believe God just wants us to be happy.

*

But the life we live in any moment, its happiness, vanishes like vapor. Like smoke. I picture you writing in a tranquil domestic interior, but if there's a concrete scene you actually make us see in your poetry it's something else: you crossing back and forth by the ruins of your burned-down house, remembering the objects and the moments now lost. *When by the ruins oft I past / My sorrowing eyes aside did cast*—in a small community, you couldn't have avoided that spot. But your words say: look, look away, look back. *My pleasant things in ashes lie, / And them behold no more shall I.* You couldn't let go of the compulsion to perceive everything that was gone. Loss is the pang that animates so much of what you wrote: what it means to know it conceptually, and then to know it more. Intimately and acutely. No matter how many volumes of history and lore you proudly held stacked inside your mind, you felt a hot wind brush past you—heard a bell chime, a mother wail—and knew how small those knowings were, clattering inside the great one.

*

It's late July here, but leaves on the trees around my house are already dry and falling. That isn't normal, is it? They crunch beneath my feet on the walkway by my house. I glance at other sidewalks as I drive through the neighborhood, wondering whether this litter of destruction is just gathering on my block, or if it's everywhere. Cicada buzz echoes the buzz inside me, an ever-present anxiety I'm afraid to keep my attention fixed on. Every time I swipe my phone it's the Day of Doom; in post after post, the red graphed line of our fate—our world's fate—rises and rises. Though my own house stands, how many others have already been destroyed by fire, by storm, by flood? Look away, look back. The world we recognize is ending around us; I don't know how much I can let myself know, I don't know how to bucket my lament. Forgive me my frailty, Anne—I am still that resolutely human fool who *takes this earth ev'n for heav'n's bower.*

*

I think how young you were when you sailed past the edge of your known world. You watched the long heave of the Atlantic, that main bar. Much of what you'd cherished swirled away in the wake. Maybe you heard in the waves what another poet would name later: *death, death, death.* Or maybe it was only how they hissed their assurance: *you cannot go back.* You'd never see your childhood home again, the well-groomed greens. I picture you standing in the beach-rubble and looking toward the horizon, knowing that in your bones. *A new world and new manners, at which my heart rose.* You meant not hope but a reeling nausea. What was left? A small store of fragile, flammable possessions. Memories. Words. Did you really convince yourself all those were vanities?

*

Nor can we go back. Not to the before-times, the before-world. Wave after wave in these past years—climate, pandemic, politics—has wiped it from us, the quaint coast of our memories, so close but vanishing. Our former selves shrunken in the retreating distance, waving their handkerchiefs. What fanciful manors we once lived in, innocent as children reciting from the epics, showing how wise we were for praise and sweetmeats. Freer than you, I can stand bare-legged with the tide pulling at my calves and ankles, feel the sea cooling them. But it makes me recall the pleasures of beach vacations I went on as a child, and I can't help contemplating how much hotter the sea is now than then, even if I can't feel the difference. Thinking of the melting ice caps, the dire hurricanes waiting to be born. Unlike you, I don't chide myself for grieving.

*

So we each sit down to write in the wrack of time, of loss, of endings. I read you in a new way now, in my own new world. Our differences as women matter less than I thought. There are these other ways in which we are linked.

*

But of course there are ways in which we are not. *Where shall I climb, sound, seek, search, or find / That* summum bonum *which may stay my mind?*—for you the question was rhetorical; you knew your answer. But I don't believe in your version of God or the heavenly house you trusted would make things up to you, so I'm groping for a solution you can't point me to. *But ah, and ah, again, my imbecility*—is there any way beyond that? Maybe there's only what you learned so well how to do in the face of your most agonizing losses: to make grief heave and turn and reach. You started here and ended there, opened the problem up, rebuked yourself to save yourself. Willed yourself on again and again toward the fragmented light. Kept the poem going until you wrestled yourself past despair. And then, let's hope, rested in it—the struggle inscribed on the paper before you, tear-stained maybe.

*

Or maybe even just listening to language. That's one thing you brought with you out of the past you never rebuked yourself for holding on to, isn't it? Nor did you seem to fear losing it. The pulse in the throat beneath the cicada buzz. The comfort of a couplet rubbing its legs, an off-rhyme clink to our modern ears in the desolate wind. Sometimes that feels as close as I'll get to something outside time—an unconditional beauty, an ineradicable happiness. *But [s]he whose name is grav'd in the white stone / Shall last and shine when all of these are gone.* That's how you ended your great poem of love for the transient world. How many years now have I kept those lines inside me, along with so many others? For you, an image lifted from Scripture and raised to mystery, a declaration of faith in immortality. For me, perhaps only the evocation of something smooth and durable I might pick up and cradle in my hand. Nonetheless, the sound of it, the feeling. Your words still here in our burning house, and you still with us, so long as we're alive to know anything. A wonderment.

Marilyn Nelson

Fair flower that for a space was lent

How dare we, the for the moment alive,
presume to question your decisions, Lord?
You've given so much more than we deserve,
tipping the scales with the thumb of vast love.

Conscious corpuscles of eternity,
we breathe in grace, and exhale gratitude,
bowing before your generosity, -
until loss strips us as naked as food.

Forgive me for questioning the wisdom
of your making a child, only to take
her after one breath back, Creator, God.
Did you waste your time? Was she a mistake?

Forgive my doubt, Lord, and help me believe
you didn't want my granddaughter to live.

Marilyn Nelson
8/30/24

Anne Bradstreet Now. Abram Van Engen and Mary Eyring, Oxford University Press.
 DOI: 10.1093/9780197811191.003.0019

James Thomas Stevens

But Yet [Her] Body is [the] Book: Haudenosaunee Women as Text

To credit seventeenth century Puritan writer, Anne Bradstreet, with being the first poet in America, based solely on publishing in print, is to ignore centuries of poetry by the Indigenous peoples of this land. In my own case, as a Kanien'kehá:ka member of the Haudenosaunee Confederacy, I look to the poetry of our recitations and ceremonies as carried and imprinted on the minds of generations of Haudenosaunee women. Though these recitations were not born from the western teachings of meter and rhyme, the natural beauty in our languages and the inherent indigenous use of metaphor would make it hard for any scholar of poetry to label it anything other. The minds of our women form our print culture, for they are imprinted with centuries of recitation.

When I read the works of Bradstreet and study the situation surrounding her publication, naturally my mind turns to the role of Puritan women in society and how different it is from the role of Haudenosaunee women. As is repeated ad nauseum in anthologies and journals, Bradstreet's first manuscript was published without her knowledge by her brother-in-law, Reverend John Woodbridge, who had taken it to London with him in 1648. Woodbridge had been called to England to facilitate negotiations between Cromwell and Charles I. American scholar, Charlotte Gordon offers a compelling argument in her essay, "Humble Assertions: The True Story of Anne Bradstreet's Publication of *The Tenth Muse*," that Bradstreet's poem, "David's Lamentation for Saul and Jonathan," a seventeenth century retelling of a bible passage that tells of King David's lamenting the deaths of his predecessor, King Saul, and his son, is a subversive response to news of the execution of Charles I by the English Puritans, which occurred in 1649, a year after Woodbridge had left for England. For "David's Lamentation" to have appeared in *The Tenth Muse*, Bradstreet would have had to get the poem to London.

Anne Bradstreet Now. Abram Van Engen and Mary Eyring, Oxford University Press.

DOI: 10.1093/9780197811191.003.0020

As a Puritan woman, Bradstreet had to reinforce her pious, dutiful, and humble persona. The claim that publication was accomplished without her knowledge helped acquit her of the sin of pride. In fact, in Woodbridge's preface to the collection, after stating that ". . . the worse effect of his [the reader's] reading will be unbelief, which will make him question whether it be a woman's work, and ask, is it possible?" He assures the reader that it is, and that it is "the fruit but of some few hours, curtailed from her sleep and other refreshments." He assures readers that the time taken to write the poems was stolen from her time of rest, after having fulfilled her daily Puritan duties.

How very different, this view of women and words from the Haudenosaunee view, where women are charged with the sacred duty of imprinting our words upon their minds. Benjamin Franklin, though speaking specifically to treaties, writes in his 1784 "Remarks Concerning the Savages of North America," "The business of the women is to take exact notice of what passes, imprint it in their memories (for they have no writing) and to communicate it to their children. *They* [my emphasis] are the records of the councils, and they preserve traditions of the stipulations in treaties 100 years back; which, when we compare with our writings, we always find exact." This same recording can be applied to ceremonial recitations as well.

One such ceremony is called in English, *The Ritual of Condolence.* This ceremony developed centuries ago in order to condole the mourning Haudenosaunee community after the death of a chief. Without going too deeply into the ritual, the grieving society is viewed as a grieving woman, a woman in need of condoling; this is accomplished by going through fifteen steps, or as western scholars of Iroquois culture label them, *articles.* The main purpose of the ceremony is ultimately to choose a new chief, but only after the process of grieving has been completed. The steps in this process address such things as the throat (not allowing it to close due to sobbing), insanity (that it may succeed a loss), and the one I shall explore, the sun (the loss of its awareness while mourning). This is the eighth *article.* This losing sight of the sun in times of great loss is a metaphor shared by both Haudenosaunee orators and the much later poet Anne Bradstreet in her poem, "Letter to Her Husband, Absent upon Publick Employment."

The following selections from the eighth section of the Condolence Ceremony are translated by nineteenth century ethnologist and philologist Horatio Hale. The language sounds dated to our twenty-first century ears and is in need of an updated translation by a mother-tongue speaker, but we can hear the metaphorical beauty. From section eight, "His Sun is Lost";

Thus it invariably comes to pass
where a great calamity has befallen a person
that the Sun is lost to that person's senses.
Then such a person knows nothing about
the movements of the Sun, nothing of its drawing
nearer and nearer to him; he is then in darkness.
Now, then, let them say it, "Now, we attach the Sun
again in its place for thee; that then shall
come to pass, when the time shall come for the
dawning of a new day; that verily thou shalt see
the Sun when it shall come up out of the horizon,
when, indeed, our Elder Brother, *the Sun,* who
lights up the earth shall come over it."

Later, Iroquois linguist and ethnographer, J.N.B. Hewitt, born on Tuscarora Indian Reservation would write: "The psychological insight of the framers of this wonderful ritualistic address is without question unsurpassed in any other composition of its kind in any other literature of the world."

Let us turn now to Bradstreet's "Letter to Her Husband, Absent upon Publick Employment." Bradstreet employs the same metaphor of the loss of the sun when mourning the absence of her husband, away for work, while she remains in Ipswich.

I, like the Earth this season, mourn in black,
My Sun is gone so far in's zodiac,
Whom whilst I 'joyed, nor storms, nor frost I felt,
His warmth such fridged colds did cause to melt.
My chilled limbs now numbed lie forlorn;
Return; return, sweet Sol, from Capricorn;
In this dead time, alas, what can I more
Than view those fruits which through thy heart I bore?

Unfortunately, we must read the Condolence selection in translation. We don't get to hear the beauty of the Kanien'kéha (Mohawk) language itself, or the prevalent anaphora, as we do in Bradstreet's poem, but we do see the similarities in their metaphorical choice. We see how the mourning/pining body fails to see or feel the sun, even though it is physically there in the sky.

We can see the need to "attach the Sun again in its place" just as Bradstreet pleads for the sun to "Return; return, sweet Sol, from Capricorn . . ." And just as the Haudenosaunee see the sun "come up out of the horizon," we see later in Bradstreet's poem that when the sun "northward to me shalt return" from the Tropics of Capricorn, it is her sincere wish that the "Sun may never set, but burn/ Within the Cancer of my glowing breast,/ The welcome house of him my dearest guest."

I return now to my original thoughts when I read the works of Anne Bradstreet, America's first published poet. There were centuries of poetic recitation by the Indigenous Nations of this continent before Bradstreet ever stepped off the *Arbella* at Salem, Massachusetts. Wisely, it was our women, our mothers, and grandmothers charged with precisely recording and storing them in the libraries of their minds. Haudenosaunee women had the agency and freedom to spend the hours they needed to remember and recite, to ensure that future generations would know the proper wording of our ways. Our women did not have to justify themselves or their time. I am reminded of a print created by Joseph Keppler titled "Savagery to "Civilization"." It appeared in *Puck* magazine in 1914, over two-hundred and fifty years after Bradstreet's book was published "without her knowledge." The print depicts a group of Haudenosaunee (Iroquois) women with blankets about their shoulders, looking over a group of well-dressed suffragettes marching with a flag that reads, "Woman Suffrage." A scroll in the bottom right lists the rights of Iroquois women: rights to the land, adoption, life and death, representation at council, etc. Beneath the image is the statement, "THE INDIAN WOMEN: We whom you pity as drudges reached centuries ago the goal that you are now nearing."

Cindy Veach

Four Quaterns for Anne Bradstreet

1.
I imagine you as a child
on Saturday's long wagon ride
to St. Botolph's Church counting your
sins, assessing how you failed Him.

I watch you adjust your wool cloak.
Imagine you as a child, lost
in thought as your sisters chatter.
What will John Cotton preach today?

Up ahead the steeple rises
above the blustery marshland.
I imagine you as a child
afraid to love the world too much.

You know your place—women, children
on one side, men on the other.
I think of all that's to come when
I imagine you as a child.

Anne Bradstreet Now. Abram Van Engen and Mary Eyring, Oxford University Press.
 DOI: 10.1093/9780197811191.003.0021

2.
You thought your smallpox was God's wrath
for your carnal passion—how you
fevered—as soon as you were well
you made amends, married Simon.

Crossing aboard the *Arbella*
you thought storms were God's punishment
for sailors who stole the ship's rum.
Ocean was sky and sky ocean.

You landed, settled and survived
the starving time yet no baby.
You thought your empty womb payback
for sins and turned to poetry.

And then a son *of vows, of tears.*
Then six years of no verse, children
your duty to God and husband.
At last, you thought, you had been blessed.

3.
Your middle years—babies, deaths, verse.
You penned your parents' epitaphs
and, afraid you'd die, wrote, *Look to*
my little babes, my dear remains.

At night you wrote down that day's lines.
Your middle years—duty and verse
that would not offend or label
you a man-like, monstrous woman.

Your sister, Sarah, sent away
for defending Anne Hutchinson.
Your middle years—prayer and verse—
saw your book, *The Tenth Muse,* published.

Your dear husband away again
you wrote, *I lead a joyless life*
and filled his void with poetry.
Your middle years—heartache, love, verse.

4.
You wanted to be remembered—
And dead, yet speak and counsel give.
You left us *your living . . . mind*, yes
pious but also feminist.

Though hope and treasure lay above
you wanted to be remembered.
Your house burned down but not your words—
Make use of what I leave in love.

You lost four grandchildren in a
row—dreamed only of joining them.
You wanted to be remembered
to leave a written legacy.

Poetry was your tool to reach
beyond the grave, pass down to us
your story, a timeless woman's
story. You have been remembered.

Notes

Quatern 1: Informed by Charlotte Gordon, *Mistress Bradstreet, The Untold Life of America's First Poet* (New York: Little, Brown and Company, 2005), Chapter 2, *Lilies and Thorns.*

Quatern 2: Informed by *Mistress Bradstreet, The Untold Life of America's First Poet* by Charlotte Gordon, Chapter 4, *A Man of Exemplary Discretion and Fidelity,* p. 48; Chapter 5, *God Is Leaving England,* p. 68; Chapter 8, *The Crossing,* p. 96; Chapter 9, *New World, New Manners,* pp. 117, 121; Chapter 10, *Upon My Son,* pp. 127, 130.

The phrase, *of vows, of tears,* is from the poem, *Upon My Son Samuel His Going for England, Nov. 6, 1657,* by Anne Bradstreet from *The Works of Anne Bradstreet,* ed. Jeannine Hensley, 3rd edition (Cambridge, MA: Harvard University Press, 2010), p. 281.

Quatern 3: The line, *Look to my little babes, my dear remains,* is from the poem, *Before the Birth of One of Her Children* by Anne Bradstreet from *The Works of Anne Bradstreet,* Jeannine Hensley, 2010 edition, p. 244.

The line, *you a man-like, monstrous woman,* is from *Mistress Bradstreet, The Untold Life of America's First Poem* by Charlotte Gordon, Chapter 11, *Enemies Within,* p. 154.

The line, *I lead a joyless life,* is from the poem, *Another* by Anne Bradstreet from *The Works of Anne Bradstreet,* Jeannine Hensley, 2010 edition, p. 251.

Quatern 4: The line, *And dead, yet speak and counsel give,* is from the poem, *In Reference to Her Children* by Anne Bradstreet from *The Works of Anne Bradstreet,* Jeannine Hensley, 2010 edition, p. 256.

The lines, *your living . . . mind,* and, *Make use of what I leave in love,* are from the poem, *To My Dear Children* by Anne Bradstreet from *The Works of Anne Bradstreet,* Jeannine Hensley, 2010 edition, p. 262.

The phrase, *dreamed only of joining them,* informed by *Mistress Bradstreet, The Untold Life of America's First Poet* by Charlotte Gordon, Chapter 18, *Farewell Dear Child,* p. 277.

The line, *to leave a written legacy,* informed by *Mistress Bradstreet, The Untold Life of America's First Poet* by Charlotte Gordon, Epilogue, *A Voice in the Wilderness,* p. 284.

G. C. Waldrep

Notes on my father's death

A / Wednesday night, 3/27

I always thought Christ would appear
to my father, as a boy, as a boy—
the new boy, and my father,
eyeing him, thinking, *I'll whup him.*

B / Thursday morning, 3/28

How normal his knuckles feel—how warm. There's no response when I ask him to squeeze, but periodically his muscles twitch.

Fast, labored breathing—the sheer exercise of it. His whole chest and face move with the effort. Both eyes are open a crack, but he's unconscious. I place my left hand in his right hand from time to time, but it seems to make no difference.

What I want to lift to God is that Christ-particle, if any, that remains inside him, from his childhood. Not from his youth or his adulthood, when he was a Methodist steward, etc. But that his grandmother and mother imparted to him when he was a child.

Perhaps that particle takes the form of John 3:16. His mother and aunts were fond of that verse, inscribed it everywhere they could. (His one maiden aunt who, after her stroke, was starved to death by the other, her sister, on a hospital bed in their home, from vengeance or sheer spite.)

I pray, silently; then I pray aloud. "Lord Jesus, that part of Thee that remains in and with my father, I lift it up to Thee."

It isn't unpleasant to rub his hand, to feel the textures of his right hand. It has been years since he was able to do much hard work, so most of the

Anne Bradstreet Now. Abram Van Engen and Mary Eyring, Oxford University Press.
 DOI: 10.1093/9780197811191.003.0022

calluses are long gone—the skin is warm and supple. His nails are cut; his hands are clean—somehow I expected they wouldn't be.

My father's beard isn't heavy, but someone must have shaved him since he was hospitalized Saturday.

A nurse comes in to administer Dilaudid, to calm his breathing. After four or five minutes it begins to work, a bit. His breathing is still labored, but it's no longer a feat of sustained gymnastics, not quite.

I lean toward him and remind him that as a child he knew Christ. As he is unconscious, this accomplishes nothing that I can discern.

I remind myself how many times that right hand has struck me, but now it is open and soft. How many times his mouth has cursed, and how it won't curse again.

When I lean close I can hear the hiss of oxygen in his cannula. It's still unclear whether he's in a light coma or merely sleeping. Perhaps that distinction doesn't matter anymore.

He has a lump on his forehead, between his right eye and his nose, not sure whether that's a result of his fall on Friday. It doesn't present as a bruise.

It occurs to me that my father has never told me any dream he had, ever. Not one, at any point in our fifty-five years together. I have no idea what he dreams, or dreamt. (Later, I will ask my mother, and she will say he never told her any dream he'd had, either.)

There are moments when I recognize him, and other moments when I don't, when the emaciated face seems unfamiliar. He could be anyone, really, lying in his hospital bed.

As I massage his hand, I feel the lens-shaped seed of an old callus deep in his palm, floating in the tissues beneath the silk-like surface of this newer, untested skin. I wonder what its origins were. Using a shovel? Driving a car? Loading a gun? It's a little memory-island of past effort.

There is no smell to him. This is the longest he has gone without smoking in seventy years.

*

11:32 a.m. It's not clear who notices first: me, holding his hand, turning to speak to my mother's garden club friend, who has just arrived (because it's visiting hours), not realizing the gravity of the situation; the friend, looking past me to my father; or the machine to which my father is tethered.

I feel the chill, sudden, in his hand, a subsidence if not a release. My mother's friend points, says "he's not breathing." At precisely the same moment the machine's warning alarm goes off and the nurses rush in. But at the moment of his death this trinity: son, mother's friend, machine.

He makes a gaunt corpse, his mouth wrenched open and to one side, as if he's trying to reach something difficult and internal with his tongue. Soon the fire will teach his body its new name.

C / The Eclipse

The off-duty ambulance slides to the signal.
I look over at the driver,
and then the driver looks over at me.

While man is man, he shall have ease or pain.

What I'm missing is an anthropology
of waiting, not durance but waiting,
the unfixed interval toward which we propose
a parenthesis which it, waiting, rejects.

It has a grammar, this rejection. It must have.

Long strands of wind unknotting,
the yew blown into the quince, the quince
back into the yew: the insolence
of light, and of the cry that precedes it,

an oath. *Or like a shadow turning as it was.*

D / After

And so we make an end. Trace and breath, those twinned pages, now loyal, now disloyal.

The mind that honors the wound
in the earth's secret trade,
and the breath receding
into the poverty of the evergreens.

Parallel orphan the breath
hails, its unvoiced ruin
among the world's true shapes.
The scar the voice quickens
across the broken surface
we climb towards, and the breath
rising to meet it, bearing before it
its unaccountable appetite.

O let me never see Thee that art
invisible, and I shall not be
unwilling to come,
though by so rough a messenger.

THE ECLIPSE

Or like a shadow turning as it was.
It rained into the torn praise
the alphabet raised from the ashes
of our fathers, all the fathers,
Christ plying the river that is
the world's great instrument, shining
inside the fretwork of lost objects.
I had been looking for morning,
for the fragrant mouth-disappearance
that signifies the gentleness
of the trout lily strapped beneath
its payload of diluted stars.
Its decumbent metaphysics, a door
that opens horizontally
into a space preserved for distance.
In all my dreams of childhood
my father is absent.
On weekends he made a sound,
sounds, as we are assured the eclipse
also does, rather than, say, winter's
oblique paraphrase, which at any rate
has itself disappeared into
the green estate. *Why are you still*
crying is not the sentence
I thought I heard, or meant to say.
I hear it still. I hear it
come to rest to one side of the yew
hedge, where the lilac is practicing
its annual fugue
above the ground-shock
of the violets, already bitten away
as if by the elsewhere of meaning,

the open throat of the text
of the withered pine in the yard
of the neighbor with the small dog
that smothers the sky
with its barking, day or night,
embedded in the lyrical ovation.

Epilogue

The truth is we do some things because we are asked to do them. Anne Bradstreet knew this well: her last prose work, "Meditations Divine and Moral," is explicitly a response to her son Simon's request "to leave something for you in writing that you might look upon, when you should see me no more." Simon's request is a trace; Anne's belated answer to his request is a trace; the text itself, like every text, is a trace.

I was asked to contribute a poem (or two) to this volume on Bradstreet, and somewhat later I was asked, by my father, to "come down now." My father, who had moderately advanced dementia, had wandered outside in the night, fallen, and lain unnoticed for twelve or thirteen hours in cold rain; he was subsequently admitted to the hospital with cuts and bruises from his fall, hypothermia, pneumonia, and sepsis. For a few days he was insensible as they warmed his body (for the hypothermia) and flooded it with antibiotics (for the sepsis). Then he had just a bit more than a day—Tuesday into Wednesday, in the chronology of the poem—of seeming more or less lucid, before slipping into a light coma (if it was that) Wednesday night.

On Tuesday I asked him, on the phone, whether I should come, and he said "no." On Wednesday, as he was being moved to hospice, I asked again, and he said "come down now."

When I read Bradstreet's poetry, I often think of it as a poetics of obligation. I don't mean "obligation" as necessarily onerous, or inauthentic. But to obligate (or be obligated) is to bind (or be bound) against, or toward: it is a tether, a responsibility.

Bradstreet was no stranger to obligation. Her verse may be construed as a set of obligatory fulfillments in relation to her God, her church, her nation, the classical tradition, her own intellect (as a God-given faculty), and the people she loved most, her family. Her body of work represents a long binding-*towards,* in language. It was both a duty and a pleasure.

I did not have Bradstreet's poems with me at my father's bedside in the hospital's hospice ward, but I did have them back at the room where I was sleeping, and I had them in my head. "The world, the useful, hurtful, and the good," Bradstreet euphonized to her father, Thomas Dudley (in what she characterized, explicitly, as "duty"). My relationship with my own father was fraught, and often violent, across a multi-generational panorama of violence (of fathers, and sons).

We write toward, or against, the obligations that tether us. To a Christian, for whom the great obligation to the resurrected Christ remains our cardinal indenture, the Christ from whom all language (as word derived from Word) flows, this is both natural and unnatural, bound and free.

On the Thursday of the poem, I sat with my unconscious father and held his hand for three hours as he lay dying. The only times I let go of his hand were to write some of these lines.

The Bradstreet line that echoed in my head that day was from a poem not to her father, but to one of her dead grandchildren: *Or like a shadow turning as it was.* The rhyme Bradstreet chooses in that couplet ("glass"/"was") is imperfect and seems to echo the fragility of both the life she mourns and her relationship with that life, that will now "ne'er . . . come to me."

The thing about the trace is that it is, by definition, perceptible. Bradstreet placed her ultimate trust in "the invisible," whom she nevertheless hoped "ever" to see. Yet in the Old Testament, to see God (or even His angels) was to court annihilation. And God in Himself is not a trace, but a Whole. In adding one letter to the closing quatrain of "Notes on my Father's Death" (construed as a quatrain although it's prose in Bradstreet's original) and thus producing a double negative, I was meditating on the difference, and distance, between the trace, which we perceive, and the invisible, which we don't.

As for the eclipse, that cosmic shadow-play, I think Bradstreet would have honored it with a poem: as a *wonder,* a visual manifestation of the ongoing commitment of God to His creation, a mediation between the infinitude of God and a creation placed in space and time.

Ultimately, "so rough a messenger" in my poem is not death arriving, but my father departing. The dying always take something with them, when they go. We may characterize the condition of acknowledging this as "grief," or (as Bradstreet does elsewhere) as "debt." Perhaps it is also one of the more difficult forms of mercy—which stands outside all obligation.

Afterword

When Anne Bradstreet anticipated responses to the poems presented in *The Tenth Muse Lately Sprung Up in America*, she worried critics would hold her at an unforgiving distance. In her poem "The Prologue," she imagined the "carping tongue[s]" of readers who would find her "obnoxious" and, as a woman, ill-suited for literary labor. Perhaps she was catastrophizing, or perhaps she wrote what she knew from circulating her manuscripts or participating in discussions of other English women's poetry. She could not imagine critics willing to be drawn in by her craft, even if her poems achieved her vision for them. "If what I do prove well, it won't advance./ They'll say it's stolen, or else, it was by chance."[1]

But she miscalculated. Yes, critics have found fault with her work. Some poets in this collection quote familiar reservations about Bradstreet's poetry and a few voice their own. Adrienne Rich calls Bradstreet's early verse "often pedestrian, abstract, mechanical."[2] Eavan Boland writes, "It would be wrong to make extravagant claims for Anne Bradstreet. Her work is memorable and strange and moving but also uneven and unrealized in certain parts."[3] John Berryman tires of the quaternions' preoccupation with "anything past, dead, far,/ sacred . . ."[4] Yet this is less critical carping than qualifying what often turns out to be rapturous praise of Bradstreet offered in the course of promoting her work. If Bradstreet was in earnest when she worried about critics refusing the advances of her writing, she might be surprised and

[1] Margaret Olofson Thickstun, ed, *Anne Bradstreet: Poems and Meditations* (Toronto, Ontario: Iter Press, 2019), 45.

[2] Adrienne Rich, "Anne Bradstreet and Her Poetry" in *The Works of Anne Bradstreet*, ed. Jeannine Hensley (Cambridge, MA: Belknap Press, 1967, 2010), xiii.

[3] Eavan Boland, "Finding Anne Bradstreet," in *Green Thoughts, Green Shades: Essays by Contemporary Poets on the Early Modern Lyric*, ed. Jonathan F. S. Post (Berkeley, CA: University of California Press, 2022), 189.

[4] John Berryman, *Homage to Mistress Bradstreet and Other Poems* (London: Faber and Faber, 1959), 14.

possibly discomfited to realize how many readers have eagerly entered the space dividing her from her audience—how deeply they have come to identify with her poetry, her prose, and the most intimate experiences of her life.

Rich, Boland, and Berryman do not simply admire Bradstreet's work; they are mesmerized by her presence. Of the subject of his long poem *Homage to Mistress Bradstreet,* Berryman said, "I did not choose her—somehow she chose me."[5] His poem explores Bradstreet's faith, her relationship to her father, and her literary labor. It probes her infertile womb and follows her, unbidden, into her bedroom. Bradstreet might have preferred critical oblivion to this homage. But modern poets sense something in Bradstreet reaching for them despite, or possibly even because of, the wintry formality of her patriarchal puritan culture. Boland writes, "The truth is, I cannot afford not to see Anne Bradstreet. She lays her claim across every boundary, in spite of every distance. What's more, she tests my own powers of reconstruction. Pock-marked, slightly lame, outspoken and astonishing in her ability to survive the odds, she comes before me."[6] In a postscript dated 1979, Rich explained and reconsidered the tepid praise of Bradstreet she offered in a 1966 foreword to Jeannine Hensley's edition of her works. "Reading and writing about Bradstreet, I began to feel that furtive, almost guilty spark of identification so often kindled in me, in those days, by the life of another woman writer," she says. "There were real parallels between her life and mine. Like her, I had learned to read and write in my father's library; like her, I had known the ambiguities of patronizing compliments from male critics; like her, I suffered from chronic lameness; but above all, she was one of the few women writers I knew anything about who had also been a mother."[7] If the portions of Bradstreet's work included in anthologies are any indication, generations of readers feel with Rich that Bradstreet's voice is most affecting in this mode, when she addresses her children with anxious concern for their welfare and wrenching honesty about what it has cost her to care for them.

Bradstreet's children are the only readers we know for certain she wanted to reach. She wrote at the beginning of her spiritual autobiography:

[5] John Berryman, "One Answer to a Question," *Shenandoah: The Washington and Lee University Review,* XVII (Autumn 1965).

[6] Boland, "Finding Anne Bradstreet," 189.

[7] Rich, "Anne Bradstreet and Her Poetry," xx–xxi.

> This book by any yet unread,
> I leave for you when I am dead,
> That being gone, here you may find
> What was your living mother's mind.
> Make use of what I leave in love,
> And God shall bless you from above.[8]

Because the writings Bradstreet left to her family resonate with modern readers more than the poems included in *The Tenth Muse*, many readers have slipped into the subject position of her children, where Bradstreet offers them sympathy for losses ranging from the material to the existential. Readers can feel Bradstreet's pain and accept her offer to commiserate. But whatever warmth they find in her company, they are not invited guests at her table. If it is difficult to ascertain Bradstreet's intended audience for *The Tenth Muse* or the verse added to *Several Poems*, it is impossible to determine how she would feel about modern responses to her personal writing. No evidence suggests she ever considered an audience outside her family when she wrote it. Kimberly Johnson remarks upon the uneasy position in which contemporary readers find themselves in relation to Bradstreet's work. "I don't want to be a kind reader of Bradstreet," she declares. "I want to be a provoked, stymied, excited, and even estranged reader. I don't want Bradstreet to be my mom; I want her to be my challenger." One can imagine Bradstreet sympathizing with and returning the sentiment. She might be put off by the notion that readers with no filial claim on her would presume to regard her as a maternal figure, or would find more resonance with her "domestic" lyrics than her demanding quaternions.

Of course, one can only imagine this. We have breached the boundary of what can be known or responsibly argued about Bradstreet. Scholars of Bradstreet must leave off where the evidence gives out—a fact they frequently lament by way of closing off tantalizing lines of inquiry about her work and worlds. We can never know, scholars remind us, why Bradstreet wrote poetry, whether she aspired to print publication, how she felt about certain political controversies or religious policies, whether her views changed over time, or why it is she chose to write about certain moments and people in her life and not others. The silences in historical archives stop scholars in their tracks. But poets can go further. They are positioned to supplement what surviving

[8] Thickstun, *Anne Bradstreet*, 304.

records tell us about Bradstreet. They need not be her children to be her relations, affiliated by the materials, intellectual demands, and emotional labor of the poetic process. They share Bradstreet's condition of writing poetry in strange and shifting worlds that too often disregard the poet's work. Because of this, they can infer, interpret, and imagine new meanings in her writing and make different kinds of claims about the value of her literary labor and productions.

This collection stands as a crucial complement to the scholarship on Bradstreet that has shaped what we know of her and that will continue, if we are fortunate, to expand and refine our understanding of Bradstreet and poetic traditions more broadly. Many of the poets included in this volume are also at the forefront of scholarship in literary studies, early modern studies, Native American and Indigenous studies, women's studies, and related fields. This collection adds not just new ways of seeing Bradstreet and her milieu but also, and perhaps more urgently, a case for the value of laboring to perceive what cannot be known about Bradstreet. The poetic imagination enables a different kind of understanding. So much of Bradstreet's experience has been beyond the reach of traditional scholarship and must remain so, not just because of impoverished archives or the distance between puritan settlements and our own environments, but because entire dimensions of her being were inconstant and inscrutable even in her day, even to her. The poets in this collection make a case for noticing in new ways, for introducing evidence that is bound to be speculative, emotional, interested, incomplete, and inconclusive—manifestations of imagination that both illuminate and respond to what has come before. And each of these pieces, in turn, invites another response. As we engage these poets and add our own voices, we carry into the future an ongoing and ever-changing conversation about the legacies and resonances of the past.

Contributors

David Baker is the author or editor of many books of poetry and poetry criticism. His most recent poetry collections are *Transit* (2026), *Whale Fall* (2022), *Swift: New and Selected Poems* (2019), *Scavenger Loop* (2015), and *Never-Ending Birds* (2009), which won the Theodore Roethke Memorial Poetry Prize in 2011. In 2025, he co-edited, with Michael Collier, *Collected Poems of Stanley Plumly*; and with Ann Townsend, he co-edited *Radiant Lyre: Essays on Lyric Poetry* in 2009. He has also written several works of literary criticism, most recently *Seek After: On Seven Modern Lyric Poets* (2018) and *Show Me Your Environment: Essays on Poetry, Poets, and Poems* (2014). Baker is the recipient of prizes and fellowships from the Guggenheim Foundation, National Endowment for the Arts, Theodore Roethke Memorial Foundation, Ohio Arts Council, Mellon Foundation, Poetry Society of America, the Pushcart Foundation, Utah Arts Council, Society of Midland Authors, and Ohioana Library Association. For more than twenty-five years, he served as Poetry Editor of *The Kenyon Review*. He is currently Professor Emeritus of English at Denison University, where since 1984 he taught courses in literature, poetics, and creative writing.

Mary Jo Bang is the author of nine books of poems, including *A Film in Which I Play Everyone*, nominated for a Lambda Literary Award and the PEN/Voelcker Award, *A Doll for Throwing*, and *Elegy*, which received the National Book Critics Circle Award. She has published translations of Dante's *Divine Comedy* and *Colonies of Paradise: Poems* by Matthias Göritz. She is also the co-translator, with Yuki Tanaka, of *A Kiss for the Absolute: Selected Poems of Shuzo Takiguchi*. She's been the recipient of a Hodder Fellowship from Princeton University, a Guggenheim Foundation Fellowship, and a Berlin Prize Fellowship from the American Academy in Berlin. She's a Professor of English at Washington University in St. Louis where she teaches creative writing.

Dan Beachy-Quick is a poet, essayist, and translator. Among his nine books of poetry are *Elements & Offerings* (2026), *Arrows* (2020), a Poetry Society of Virginia North American Book Award Semifinalist; *Variations on Dawn and Dusk* (2019), which was longlisted for the 2019 National Book Award for Poetry; *Circle's Apprentice* (2011), winner of the 2012 Colorado Book Award; and *Mulberry* (2006), a finalist for the *Los Angeles Times* Book Award for poetry. He has published three translated poetry collections: *Wind—Mountain—Oak: The Poems of Sappho* (2023), *The Thinking Root: The Poetry of the Earliest Greek Philosophy* (2023), and *Stone-Garland: Six Poets from the Greek Lyric Tradition* (2020). Among his many other works are a collection of essays, fragments, and poems, *Of Silence and Song* (2017), and *A Whaler's Dictionary* (2008), interlinked essays which respond to the form and themes of *Moby-Dick*. He has been a finalist for the William Carlos Williams Award and the PEN/USA Literary Award in Poetry, and is the recipient of a Lannan Foundation Residency and a Guggenheim Fellowship. He lives in Colorado, where he is University Distinguished Teaching Scholar at Colorado State University.

Kimberly L. Becker is the author of six poetry collections. She has also published creative nonfiction, most recently in *Unpapered: Writers Consider Native American Identity and Cultural Belonging* (2023). Her poetry collections include *Words Facing East* (2010), *The Dividings* (2014), *Flight* (2018), *The Bed Book* (2020), *Bringing Back the Fire* (2022), and *Rivering* (2025). She has been widely published in journals and anthologies, including *Indigenous Message on Water*, *Women Write Resistance: Poets Resist Gender Violence*, and *Tending the Fire: Native Voices and Portraits*. She has received a number of grants and has held residencies at Hambidge, Weymouth, and Wildacres. She has served as mentor for PEN America's Prison Writing and AWP's Writer to Writer programs. Her work has been honored with awards including a nomination for a Pushcart prize.

Sophie Cabot Black has four poetry collections: *The Misunderstanding of Nature*, which won the Poetry Society of America's Norma Faber First Book Award; *The Descent*; *The Exchange*; and most recently, *Geometry of the Restless Herd*. Her poetry has appeared in numerous magazines, including *The Atlantic Monthly*, *The New Republic*, *The New Yorker*, and *The Paris Review*.

Eavan Boland (1944–2020) was a Dublin-born poet, critic, and teacher who became an influential voice in modern Irish literature. Boland's poetry collections include *A Poet's Dublin* (2014); *A Woman Without a Country* (2014); *New Collected Poems* (2008); *An Origin Like Water: Collected Poems 1967–1987* (1996); and *In Her Own Image* (1980), among other books. She is also the author of several essay collections and an autobiographical volume called *Object Lessons: The Life of the Woman and the Poet in Our Time* (1995). For her work, Boland was made an honorary member of the Royal Irish Academy, the American Academy of Arts and Sciences, and the Irish Academy of Letters. She received the Lifetime Achievement Award at the Irish Book Awards in 2017.

Daniel Borzutzky is a poet and translator, and the author of *The Performance of Becoming Human*, winner of the 2016 National Book Award for Poetry. He holds a joint appointment as LAS Distinguished Professor of English and Latin American and Latino Studies at the University of Illinois, Chicago. His other books include *The Murmuring Grief of the Americas* (2024), *Written After a Massacre in the Year 2018* (2021), *Lake Michigan* (2018), which was a finalist for the Griffin International Poetry Prize, *In the Murmurs of the Rotten Carcass Economy* (2015), and *The Book of Interfering Bodies* (2011). He has also translated many books. His translation of Galo Ghigliotto's *Valdivia* won the 2017 National Translation Award, and his translation of *The Loose Pearl* by Paula Ilabaca Nuñez (2022) won the Pen Award for Poetry in

Translation. Other translations include Raúl Zurita's *The Country of Planks* and *Song for His Disappeared Love*, Jaime Luis Huenún's *Port Trakl*, and most recently *The Deer Book* by Cecilia Vicuña (2024).

Eduardo C. Corral is the author of two books of poetry. The first, *Slow Lightning* (2012), won the Yale Series of Younger Poets competition. His second, *Guillotine*, was published in 2020. His poems have appeared in *Ambit, New England Review, The New Republic, Ploughshares*, and *Poetry*. His work has been honored with residencies from the MacDowell Colony, Yaddo, and Civitella Ranieri. Among his many awards are a Whiting Writers' Award and a National Endowment for the Arts Fellowship. He has also received the Hodder Fellowship and the National Holmes Poetry Prize from Princeton University. He teaches at Washington University in St. Louis.

Joanne Diaz is a poet and literary scholar. She is the author of three books of poetry: *The Lessons* (2011), winner of the Gerald Cable First Book Award, *My Favorite Tyrants* (2014), winner of the Brittingham Prize, and *Electric Dress*, winner of the Barrow Street Editors Prize (2026). With Ian Morris, she is the co-editor of *The Little Magazine in Contemporary America*, a collection of reflections and insights offered by prominent editors of flourishing small-circulation magazines. She is also the co-host, with Abram Van Engen, of the *Poetry for All* podcast. Her scholarship focuses on archives, book history, and the poetry and drama of Shakespeare and his contemporaries. She has received fellowships from the National Endowment for the Arts, the Illinois Arts Council, the Sustainable Arts Foundation, and the Bread Loaf Writers Conference. She is the Isaac Funk Professor of English at Illinois Wesleyan University.

Kathy Fagan's newest collection of poems is *The Unbecoming*, published by Norton in September 2026. Her book, *Bad Hobby*, won the 2023 William Carlos Williams Award, and her others include *The Raft* (1985), a National Poetry Series Award winner; *MOVING & ST RAGE* (1999), winner of the Vassar Miller Prize for Poetry; *The Charm* (2002); *Lip* (2009); and *Sycamore* (2017), for which she was awarded Ohio Poet of the Year. Her poetry has appeared in publications such as *Poetry, The Atlantic, The Paris Review, FIELD, The Kenyon Review, Slate, The New York Times*, and *The Nation*. Her awards include fellowships from the the Guggenheim Foundation, the NEA, the Ingram Merrill Foundation, the Frost Place, and the Ohio Arts Council. Fagan served as co-editor of the Wheeler Poetry Prize Book Series for *The Journal* and The Ohio State University Press for thirty-five years and is Professor Emerita at The Ohio State University, where she co-founded the MFA Program.

Rigoberto González is the author of eighteen books of poetry and prose, most recently *To the Boy Who Was Night: Poems, Selected and New* (2023), an autobiographical meditation. González has also edited several books, including *Camino del Sol: 15 Years of Latina and Latino Writing* (2010) and *Latino Poetry* (2024) from the Library of America. His awards include Lannan, Guggenheim, NEA, NYFA, and USA Rolón fellowships, the American Book Award, the Lambda Literary Award, the Shelley

Memorial Prize from the Poetry Society of America, the Lenore Marshall Prize from the Academy of American Poets, and PEN/ Voelcker Award for Poetry. He recently won the Poetry Foundation's Ruth Lilly Poetry Prize for lifetime achievement. González is Professor and Director of Creative Writing at Rutgers University.

Linda Gregerson is the Caroline Walker Bynum Distinguished University Professor Emerita at the University of Michigan and is the author of seven volumes of poetry, most recently *Canopy* (2022) and *Prodigal: New and Selected Poems* (2015). Her second book of poems, *The Woman Who Died in Her Sleep* (1996), was a finalist for both the Poet's Prize and the Lenore Marshall Poetry Prize. *Waterborne* (2002) won the Kingsley Tufts Poetry Award; *Magnetic North* (2007) was a finalist for the National Book Award. Her works of literary criticism include *The Reformation of the Subject: Spenser, Milton, and the English Protestant Epic* (1995) *and Negative Capability: Contemporary American Poetry* (2001). She has published numerous essays on Renaissance literature and culture, and on twentieth- and twentieth-first century lyric poetry. Among her prizes and honors are awards from the American Academy of Arts and Letters, the Poetry Society of America, the Modern Poetry Association, the National Humanities Center, the Institute for Advanced Study, the National Endowment for the Arts, the Guggenheim, Mellon, and Rockefeller Foundations. Gregerson is a fellow of the American Academy of Arts and Sciences and a former Chancellor of the Academy of American Poets. She divides her time between Ann Arbor and London.

Niki Herd is the author of two collections of poetry, most recently *The Stuff of Hollywood* (2024), finalist for a Lambda Literary Award and longlisted for the Maya Angelou Book Award, and *The Language of Shedding Skin* (2011). She is the co-editor of *Laura Hershey: On the Life & Work of an American Master*. A three-time Pushcart Prize nominee, her work has been supported by MacDowell, Ucross, the Bread Loaf Writers' Conference, the Newberry Library, and Cave Canem. She's a contributing editor for *Copper Nickel* and her poetry, scholarship, and essays have been published in the *New England Review*, the Academy of American Poets Poem-a-Day, the *Oxford Research Encyclopedia of Literature*, and *Salon*, among others. She has taught at the University of Houston and Washington University in St. Louis. Herd is currently an assistant professor at Franklin & Marshall College.

Kimberly Johnson is a poet, translator, and scholar of early modern literature. She is the author of four books of poetry: *Fatal* (2022), *Uncommon Prayer* (2014), *A Metaphorical God* (2008), and *Leviathan with a Hook* (2002), and of a critical monograph, *Made Flesh: Sacrament and Poetics in Post-Reformation England* (2014), which considers how the poetic practice of seventeenth-century writers such as John Donne, George Herbert, and Edward Taylor was informed by the interpretive problem of the Eucharist. She is the co-editor, with Jay Hopler, of *Before the Door of God: An Anthology of Devotional Poetry* (2013) and has served as editor on five volumes of literary criticism. Her translation of Virgil's *Georgics* appeared in 2009 and her translation of Hesiod's *Theogony & Works and Days* in 2017. Her work has appeared in a variety of publications, including *The New Yorker, Slate, The Iowa Review, The Sewanee Review, PMLA,* and *Modern Philology.* Her work has been honored and supported with grants from the Guggenheim Foundation, the National Endowment for the Arts, the Utah Arts Council, and the Amy Lowell Trust. She is currently Professor of English at Brigham Young University, where she teaches early modern literature and creative writing.

John Keene is the author of a handful of books, including *Punks: New & Selected Poems* (2021), winner of the 2022 National Book Award for Poetry, a Lambda Literary for Gay Poetry and the Thom Gunn Award, *Seismosis* (2006), an art-text collaboration with the artist Christopher Stackhouse, the poetic novel *Annotations* (1995) and the short fiction collection *Counternarratives* (2015), which won the inaugural Republic of Consciousness Prize for Small Presses, an American Book Award, the Lannan Literary Award for fiction, and the Windham-Campbell Prize in Fiction. His other published work includes *GRIND* (2016), an art-text collaboration with photographer Nicholas Muellner, and the poetry chapbook *Playland* (2016). With Robert F. Reid-Pharr he co-edited *Love Is a Dangerous Word: Selected Poems* by Essex Hemphill (2025). His translation from the Portuguese of Hilda Hilst's novel *Letters from a Seducer* was published in 2014, and republished in a revised edition in 2025. In 2018 he received a MacArthur "Genius" Fellowship. He serves as fiction and hybrid writing editor for *Obsidian* and as a Contributing Editor for the *James Baldwin Review.* He is Board of Governors Professor of English and Distinguished Professor of English and Africana Studies at Rutgers University-Newark, where he also teaches in the MFA in Creative Writing Program.

Karen An-hwei Lee is a poet, novelist, literary critic, and translator. She is the author of six books of poetry: *The Beautiful Immunity* (2024); *Duress* (2022); *Rose is a Verb: Neo-Georgics* (2021); *Phyla of Joy* (2012); *Ardor* (2008), a July Open selection; and *In Medias Res* (2004), winner of the Kathryn A. Morton Prize and the Norma Farber First Book Award. She is the author of four novels: *Sonata in K* (2017); *The Maze of Transparencies* (2019); *Love Chronicles of the Octopodes* (2023); and *Marimo, Mon Amour* (2026), winner of the Catherine Doctorow Prize for Innovative Fiction. She has written a work of literary criticism, *Anglophone Literatures in the Asian Diaspora: Literary Transnationalism and Translingual Migrations.* She is the translator of *Doubled Radiance: Poetry & Prose of Li Qingzhao* (2018). She is the recipient of the Glenna Luschei *Prairie Schooner* Award and a fellowship from the National Endowment for the Arts. She has taught in a number of writing programs, including the Kundiman Asian American Poetry Retreat hosted by Fordham University in New York City. Currently, she serves in the administration at Wheaton College, where she is Provost and Professor of English.

Shane McCrae is the author of eight books of poetry: *Cain Named the Animal* (2022), which was shortlisted for the Forward Prize for Best Collection and nominated for the PEN/Voelcker Award; *Sometimes I Never Suffered* (2020), which was shortlisted for the 2020 T. S. Eliot Prize; *The Gilded Auction Block* (2019); *In the Language of My Captor* (2017), winner of the Anisfield-Wolf Book Award for poetry and finalist for the National Book Award; *The Animal Too Big to Kill* (2015), winner of the Lexi Rudnitsky Editor's Choice Award; *Forgiveness Forgiveness* (2014); Blood (2013); and *Mule* (2011), winner of the PEN/USA Literary Award in Poetry and a finalist for the Kate Tufts Discovery Award. He is also the author of several chapbooks and a memoir, *Pulling the Chariot of the Sun: A Memoir of a Kidnapping* (2023). He has been awarded the Lannan Literary Award, a Whiting Writer's Award, a Guggenheim Fellowship, a fellowship from the National Endowment for the Arts, a Puschcart Prize, and the Arthur Rense Poetry Prize from the Academy of Arts and Letters. He is Poetry Editor of *Image* and an Associate Professor in the Columbia University MFA Writing Program.

Anne Myles is a poet and scholar of early modern literature. Her debut full-length collection of poems, *Late Epistle,* was winner of Sappho's Prize in Poetry (Headmistress Press, 2023). Her chapbook, *What Woman That Was: Poems for Mary Dyer* (2022), is a sequence of 28 poems contemplating the life of the seventeenth-century New England Quaker martyr Mary Barrett Dyer. As a literary scholar, she has taught, researched, and published on early American life and literature, with a focus on New England religious dissenters and queer readings. Her scholarly work has appeared in *Early American Literature, Feminist Studies, William & Mary Quarterly,* and essay collections including *Long Before Stonewall: Same-Sex Sexualities in Early America,* edited by Thomas Foster (2007). After a distinguished academic career, Myles began publishing poetry in 2018. She is Professor Emeritus of English at the University of Northern Iowa and received her MFA from the Vermont College of Fine Arts.

Marilyn Nelson is the author, co-author, or translator of more than thirty books for children and adults. Her books of poetry include *For the Body* (1978); *The Homeplace* (1990), a finalist for the National Book Award; and *The Fields of Praise: New and Selected Poems* (1997), winner of the Poets' Prize and a finalist for the National Book Award. Among her acclaimed books for young readers are *Carver: A Life in Poems* (2001), a finalist for the National Book Award and recipient of the Boston Globe/Horn Book Award, a Newbery Honor designation, a Coretta Scott King Honor Book designation, and the Flora Stieglitz Straus Award for Nonfiction; *Fortune's Bones: The Manumission Requiem* (2004), winner of the Coretta Scott King Book Award; and *A Wreath for Emmett Till* (2005), designated a Michael L. Printz Award honor book, a Lee Bennett Hopkins Poetry Award honor book, and recipient of a Coretta Scott King Honor Award. Her translated works include *The Thirteenth Month* by Inge Pedersen and Euripides' *Hecuba.* Among her honors are two fellowships from the National Endowments of the Arts, the 1990 Connecticut Arts Award, a Guggenheim Fellowship, the Connecticut Book Awards Lifetime Achievement Honor, the NSK Neustadt Prize for Children's Literature, the Frost Medal, and the Ruth Lilly Poetry Prize. From 2001 to 2006, she was poet laureate of the State of Connecticut. In 2013, she was elected a Chancellor of the Academy of American Poets. She was the founder and director of Soul Mountain Retreat and is Professor Emeritus of English at the University of Connecticut.

James Thomas Stevens is a member of the Akwesasne Mohawk Nation who also publishes under his Mohawk name, Aronhió:ta's. He is the author of nine books of poetry: *Tokinish* (1994), *Combing the Snakes from His Hair* (2002), *(dis)Orient* (2005), *Mohawk/Samoa: Transmigrations*, with Caroline Sinavaiana (2005), *Bulle/ Chimére* (2006), *The Mutual Life* (2006), *A Bridge Dead in the Water* (2007), *Of Kingdoms & Kangaroo* (2008), and *The Golden Book* (2021). His work has been widely anthologized in many venues and has been honored with awards including the City of Santa Fe Writing Award, the Wittner-Bynner Foundation Poetry Grant, and the Whiting Writers Award. He has been nominated for a Before Columbus/ American Book Award, and he was a finalist for the 2005 National Poetry Series Award. He is currently a Full Professor of creative writing at the Institute of American Indian Arts.

Cindy Veach is the author of three poetry collections: *Monster Galaxy*, a finalist for the Sally Albiso Award; *Her Kind*, an Eric Hoffer Montaigne Medal finalist; and *Gloved Against Blood*, a finalist for the Paterson Poetry Prize and a Massachusetts Center for the Book "Must Read." She is also the author of the chapbook *Innocents* and co-author, with J. D. Scrimgeour, of the script *Imprisoned! 1692* produced by the Essex National Heritage Commission. Her work has been anthologized and published in venues including The Academy of American Poets Poem-a-Day, *AGNI, Poet Lore, The North American Review, The Journal, Chicago Review,* and elsewhere. She is the recipient of the Philip Booth Poetry Prize (selected by Mary Ruefle), and her sonnet crown, "Witch Kitsch," was selected by Marilyn Nelson for the New England Poetry Club's Samuel Washington Allen Prize. She has served as assistant poetry editor for *Northwest Review* and is currently the poetry editor for *MER* (*Mom Egg Review*).

G. C. Waldrep is a poet and historian. As a poet, he is the author of seven books: *The Earliest Witness* (2021); *feast gently* (2018), winner of the William Carlos Williams Award; a long poem, *Testament* (2015); *Your Father on the Train of Ghosts* (2011), a collaboration with John Gallaher; *Archicembalo* (2009), winner of the Dorset Prize and the Alice Fay Di Castagnola Award; *Disclamor* (2007); and *Goldbeater's Skin* (2003), winner of the Colorado Prize. He is the author of several chapbooks, the most recent of which is *Susquehanna* (2013). He is the co-editor, with Ilya Kaminsky, of *Homage to Paul Celan* (2011), and the co-editor, with Joshua Corey, of *The Arcadia Project: North American Postmodern Pastoral* (2012). He is the author of a historical monograph, *Southern Workers and the Search for* Community, which examines the lives of Southern textile workers during the early twentieth century. His awards include prizes, grants, and residencies from the National Endowment for the Arts, the Lannan Foundation, the Academy of American Poets, the Poetry Society of America, the Campbell Corner Foundation, the North Carlina Arts Council, the MacDowell Colony, and Yaddo. From 2007 to 2018 he served as Editor-at-Large for *The Kenyon Review*, and from 2011 to 2021 he served as editor of *West Branch*. In 2021 he was a Visiting Fellow at Clare Hall, University of Cambridge. In 2025, he retired as Professor of Creative Writing from Bucknell University.